the complete guide to

Philippines

CFW Guidebooks
Published by CFW Publications Limited
130 Connaught Road C Hong Kong

© CFW Publications Limited, 1981
Printed in Hong Kong

PHOTO CREDITS
Nik Wheeler: Pages 43, 61

ACKNOWLEDGEMENTS
The Publishers wish to acknowledge the help given by the following
organisations in facilitating the photography for this book:
Bureau of National and Foreign Information, Manila;
Panamin, Manila; The Ministry of Tourism, Manila;
Philippine Airlines (Domestic Division), Manila.

ISBN 962 7031 06 2

the complete guide to

Philippines

by Saul Lockhart

Photography: Alain Evrard

CFW GUIDEBOOKS
Hong Kong

Contents

THE PHILIPPINES

PHILIPPINE SEA

CATANDUANES

Legazpi

Naga

Daet

MARINDUQUE

SIBUYAN SEA

Lucena

LAGUNA DE BAY

Aparri

Cagayan

Tuguegarao

River

Bagabag

Solano

LUZON

Cabanatuan

Quezon City

MANILA

Bontoc

Baguio

Tarlac

Angeles

MANILA BAY

Batangas

Calapan

MINDORO

Bongabon

Laoag

Vigan

San Fernando

Dagupan

Olongapo

SOUTH CHINA SEA

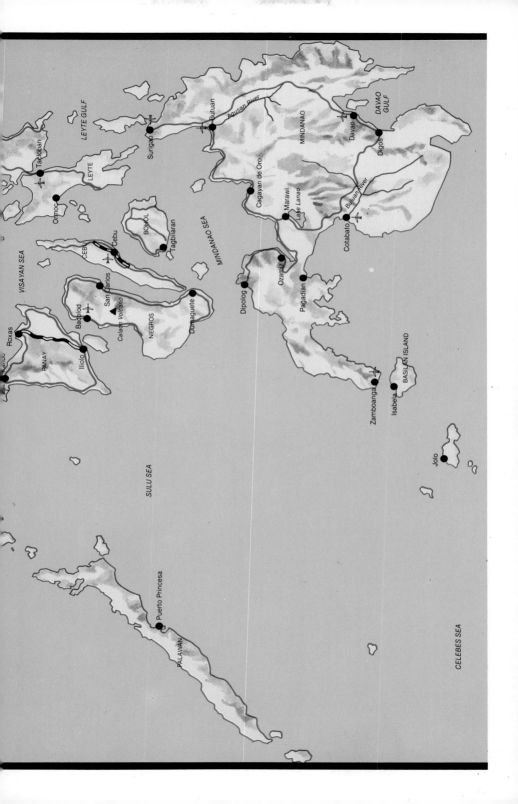

7,000 Islands
The Physical Philippines

A goddess of unparalleled beauty and purity is said to have created the Philippines by randomly flinging a handful of pearls into the empty sea — whereupon the islands sprang into being like 7,000 simultaneous births of Venus. Whether she acted merely from artless maidenly caprice or in accordance with some divine plan beyond imagination is not recorded by legend. The scientists of the less romantic present propound the antithesis of the pearl theory. The islands are now believed to be the peaks and highland plateaux of a vast submerged mountain range, a land-mass which once formed part of the Asian mainland.

The great inundation began during the last Ice Age, half a million years ago. There is botanical and zoological evidence that in more recent times at least four major land-bridges conjoined not only the three main island groups but also connected them via Borneo through what is now Indonesia to the Malayan peninsula, New Guinea and Australia; and through the Bataan islands and Taiwan to China. Massive volcanic eruptions as the earth was being formed, followed by glacial surges which preceeded the final deluge have resulted in what is officially described as "the seven major and 7,107 minor islands" that make up the Republic of The Philippines. Less than a third are inhabited or even named and the largest eleven comprise 96 percent of the total land area of 30,000 square kilometres.

The archipelago stretches about 1,690 kilometres from north to south and 1,062 kilometres broad. The northernmost tip is 240 kilometres south of Taiwan and the southernmost only 30 kilometres east of Borneo. Circumscribe a map of the country by a single line and an ovoid is formed resembling an egg in which nestles an unborn chick. This happens to be The Philippines' national and unique dish — *balut*.

Like Roman Gaul, The Philippines is usually divided into three parts: Luzon and Mindoro to the north; in the centre Visayas which includes Samar, Panay, Negros, Cebu, Leyte, and Bohol; and to the south Mindanao, the string of Sulu islands, and Palawan in the south-west. Each region contains a host of smaller islands. The first two are predominately Catholic and Western-influenced in their culture and traditions. The latter is strongly Arab-influenced with Muslim majorities and tribal minorities hidden away in mountain and forest enclaves.

Some scholars assert that primitive man may have first reached The Philippines as long ago as 75,000 years; others reduce this estimate to around 25,000 years. About 10,000 BC three separate groups appear to have been occupying the country. Two, having travelled from the east, are ethnically linked to other south and south-east Asian aborigines; the third came from the south and may be Australoid. By 5,000 BC the last of the land-bridges had disappeared beneath the sea and subsequent arrivals were more sophisticated peoples who roamed the Pacific in fleets of canoes. The

overwhelming majority of modern Filipinos descend from these groups. They displayed remarkable endurance and seamanship and are generally differentiated from the original "crude, squat, brutish and black" inhabitants by descriptions such as "tall, slender, skilled and honey-coloured." There remain unhappy echoes of this racial division even today.

For almost 2,000 years, successive waves of migration continued across the Celebes Sea and from Indo-China across the South China Sea, ending only with the arrival of the Spaniards in the 16th century. Arab traders and adventurers had preceded the Europeans by almost

200 years and, when Ferdinand Magellan sailed into Philippine waters in 1521, they exerted significant economic and cultural influence in the south. There is speculation that, as far back as the 4th century, sailing junks from China may have made occasional visits to the scattered, isolated communities which then existed. Certainly, two-way trade between China and The Philippines was conducted on a regular basis during the Tang dynasty (618-907) and increased in volume during the succeeding Sung dynasty (960-1127). Trading with Indo-China seems to have become established in the 10th century.

The migration and intermarriage of disparate races, ancient trading contacts, the immemorial pursuits of seafarers and travellers, and perhaps the elusive magic of the islands themselves have contributed to a racial mix of unusual beauty, exuberance and charm. Filipinos are an easy-going people notable for their ability to welcome any visitor, regardless of nationality, with genuine warmth.

Left, *two young* badjaos *(sea gypsies) from the island of Si Tankay, Tawi-tawi are very obliging for a tourist's camera.* Above, *stretching across northern Luzon, the Sierra Madre mountain chain separates Cagayan Valley from the Ilocos regions.*

Haciendas and Honky-Tonk
The Cultural Philippines

The Philippines is Asia's sole Christian nation, with over 80 percent of the population professing the religion, and a flourishing indigenous church. But Islam preceded Christianity by almost two centuries and, despite discouragement and occasional oppression, still claims most of the balance among the faithful. Western colonial rule was imposed on this country for longer than any other; there is equally the longest history of struggle against it. There are, indeed, elements in the national character today which reflect the essentially contradictory heritage of more than three centuries of Spanish arrogance and complacent exploitation, followed by four decades of American paternalism and benevolence not entirely free from self-interest. But that is not the whole story.

When the Portugese navigator, Ferdinand Magellan, in the employ of the Spanish throne, made his first landfall at tiny Homonhon island in the western Visayas on March 16, 1521, Philippines' gold, amber and coral had been traded for many centuries for products as varied as spices, cotton, tools, beads, silk and utensils from China, India, Persia, Venice, The Netherlands, Arabia and Indo-China. Even today it is not uncommon to find mountain tribesmen in northern Luzon with Sung, Tang and Ming Chinese export porcelain which has been in the family or tribe for countless generations.

Although the Arabian scholar, Middum, who visited the archipelago in the 14th century, is generally credited with laying the groundwork for the propogation of Islam from the most pious motives, later arrivals were spurred as

much by the rewards of commerce as by missionary zeal. Nevertheless, by the close of the 14th century Sulu Island had become the first major Islamic centre. Less than 100 years later the Johore-based Maguindana Sultanate had vastly extended the territories of Islam northwards, and the port of Manila had developed into an independent sultanate.

Magellan continued his exploration of the islands and decided to settle temporarily for provisioning and rest at the trading port of Zubu (now Cebu), where the ruler was friendly. After his great feat of endurance and seamanship, his single-minded determination, and the many perils he had encountered, it is ironic that Magellan met his death when his party became unnecessarily embroiled in a purely local conflict between the Zubu ruler and a rival chieftain, Lapu Lapu, from neighbouring Mactan Island.

Between 1525 and 1542, four separate expeditions were dispatched to The Philippines, each failing in their twin objectives of plundering the spices then thought to exist in prolific abundance and of creating a colonial presence to the glory and profit of Spain. This was not convincingly established until the arrival in 1565 of the fifth expedition, under the command of Miguel Lopez de Legazpi.

By 1570 he had reached Manila where he unexpectedly encountered "heroic defences." It took him a full year of fierce fighting before he was able to defeat the sultan, Rajah Sulaiman, and begin the establishment of the new colony's premier settlement on one of the world's great natural harbours. Manila was soon thereafter honoured by the crown with the title "Insigne y Siempre Leal Ciudad" — distinguished and ever-loyal city. It is to Legazpi that the Filipinos owe the name of their country. Originally bestowed on Samar Island by the commander of the fourth expedition in honour of crown-prince Philip of Asturias, later King Philip II of Spain, the indefatigable Legazpi succeeded in extending the name to cover the entire archipelago.

With the conquistadores came the padres. Fanning out from their powerful Manila base, the men of war pursued the goal of military victory as the men of peace dispensed the holy word and saved the heathen from eternal damnation. Not uncommonly merely a show of force, a negotiated agreement, or a timely miracle secured the domination of the Spanish crown. The cross complemented the sword, and myths of divine invincibility began to spread through the land. Many still believe today that it was not the armed might of the conquistadores and the cannons of the fleet which secured Magellan his friendly reception at Zubu. Rather, it was the image of the Christ-Child which accompanied the landing party, the sight of which instantly converted king, queen and subjects. Gradually, through the perserverance of clever padres, images of Santo Nino began replacing the existing pagan, shamanistic idols. Few Catholic homes are without such a statue today, however humble, and special veneration is afforded, and powers attributed to it.

Paradoxically, as Spain's fortunes as a world power were ebbing as the 17th became the 18th century, her colonial sway over The Philippines was consolidated. The colony was styled a "subsidiary" of Mexico, through which all trade was channelled to Spain. Galleons, which the British managed to intercept with more success than similarly intentioned Dutch attempts to blockade Manila, carried gold outward-bound and returned with cargoes of silver and consumer products. The fabled spices, which had been the original lure, always eluded them.

But the late 18th and early 19th centuries saw increasing local resentment against the harsh injustice of Spanish rule. A nascent spirit of nationalism led to over a hundred separate and more serious attempts at insurrection, each quelled by a corresponding escalation of brutality.

Opposite, *a procession of the Virgin Mary with a Moslem mosque in the background in Quiapo, a district of Manila.*

Execution — by firing-squad or garotte
— became frequent and further
exascerbated revolutionary ardour.
Forced conversion had been the practice
throughout Spanish rule, but a 1849
decree requiring the adoption of
Christian, Spanish names by all natives
served as a catalyst for yet another
rebellion.

A secret nationalist society,
Katipunan, was formed in 1892 under the
leadership of Andres Bonifacio. The
response was hundreds more executions,
among them the gentle physician, writer,
and leader of a non-violent reform
movement — Dr. Jose Rizal — in what

is now Rizal Park in central Manila on
December 30, 1896, now a national
holiday. On the day before his execution
he married his Irish Sweetheart, and just
before his death wrote her a beautiful
poem, "Mi Ultimo Adios," which
Filipinos justifiably love to recite. Rizal's
eloquent martyrdom sparked the
consolidation of the various factions
opposing the Spanish so that, after some
prevarication and the inevitable intrigue,
Emilio Aguinaldo was able to declare
independence in June 1898 and was
inaugurated as the country's first
president in January, the following year.

The elation caused by these events was

precipitating another four years of bloodshed, which subsided only in 1902.

McKinley's words may have revealed a slight ignorance of history, but they were taken literally. The goal of absolute conquest and total conversion had eluded the Spanish, despite the long duration of their stay. The inaccessibility of the northern Luzon hilltribes had kept them in ignorance of the holy word until American Protestants with exceptional fervour succeeded where the intrepid padres had failed. But even the American missionaries could not Christianise the south, where the Spanish never held more than nominal suzerainty. The Moslems remained steadfast to their belief, and Mindanao remains today the troubled bastion of Islam in the Christian Philippines.

A story is told of America's first experience in the south. The Moro people still take great pride in the fact that they were never vanquished by Spain. When General John Pershing assumed command of the Mindanao garrison in 1901 and was about to plant the U.S. flag outside his headquarters, he was confronted by a delegation of Moro chiefs. They requested he plant the flag not in the ground but on the roof: "Your buildings are yours, and on them you may fly whatever flag you wish. But the land is ours, was ours, and always will be ours." The general agreed. The possible reaction of his Spanish counterpart of a different era can only be a matter for conjecture.

American rule proved kinder than that of their predecessors. In 1907 a Philippines Assembly was set up as "a partnership in democracy," a daring experiment for any colonial power. Universal education to university level was introduced, whereas the Spanish had restricted this privilege to the religious

short-lived. Without consulting the government of the fledgeling republic, the U.S. fleet, commanded by Admiral George Dewey, sailed into Manila Bay to claim the islands under the terms of the settlement of the Spanish-American war. A fierce sea battle between the two fleets resulted in the Americans emerging victorious. The citizens of Manila are reported to have "cheered wildly" at the outcome, but again the exultance was brief. Dewey informed Washington: "We have taken the Philippines. What shall we do with them?" President McKinley responded: "Educate . . . uplift and civilise and christianise them . . ." —

Rulers of the Philippines since 1972, President Marcos and Madame Imelda R. Marcos review the festivities at the celebration of Philippine Independence at the Luneta Park in Manila.

and the elite. Roads were built; health, transport and communications facilities improved; the economy modernised; and industry activated.

An Act of Congress created the Commonwealth of The Philippines in 1935, assuring independence within a decade. Manuel Quezon was inaugurated as president the next year, but the well-planned path to independence was disrupted when Japan invaded in December 1941, two days after Pearl Harbour. General Douglas MacArthur, commanding the U.S. forces (into which those of The Philippines had been incorporated) returned, as promised, in October 1944, and complete liberation was achieved within a year. In July 1946 President Manuel Roxas assumed office, ending America's principal colonial adventure.

From 1946 until 1972 when the incumbent president, Ferdinand Marcos, declared martial law in the face of mounting anarchy, democratic elections were held as scheduled every four years — in the American style, but with much greater passion and violence. The media, proudly described as the freest in Asia, certainly the most interesting, and possibly the most outrageously libellous, contributed to the political tumult. Since the 1950s the army has been engaged in combating leftist insurgencies, centred in Luzon, and armed intransigence from the Muslims of the south. At the time of writing, President Marcos continues to head a martial law administration. The Philippines is a member of ASEAN; has two major American military bases on its soil; and normally adopts a pro-Western stance in foreign policy.

It would be difficult for a Filipino to dismiss the Spanish influence as all bad when Catholicism has been embraced with such whole-hearted enthusiasm. From Spain may have come, or have reinforced, the appreciation of the langorous pace of hacienda life; the charming, if sometimes frustrating, attitude of *mañana*; the love of fiesta, lavish hospitality, display and formal

promenade; and civilised eating and drinking habits. But there is also the pride that can be too quick to take offence; the irrational bravado of a poor man spending his last pesos on a new shirt or flashy trinket; and the vanity of the constant gazer into mirrors.

From America may have come the flare for individual enterprise; the sincere desire for education and belief in personal liberty; and a refreshing sense of the intrinsic equality of all men. Against which could be placed the ruthless pursuit of self-advantage, regardless of the consequence to others; and blatantly self-seeking commercialism.

One writer has described the result of the dual colonial influence as "a curious mix of American honky-tonk under a thin Spanish veil of Spanish Catholicism and tradition." But there is no resignation to poverty in The Philippines, and violence, born of frustration, lurks close to the surface. It is tempered by a disposition characterised by good-nature and good-humour, which may be innate and have little or no bearing on the former overlords.

Smile at a Filipino in the street and he will always respond with a friendly grin of his own. Try that in New York or Madrid.

Centre, above, *the Philippines' answer to Mardi Gras is the exhuberant* Ati-Atihan *festival held annually in Kalibo, Aklan.*

Filipino Fiesta
Prayer and Pageantry at the Mardis Gras

That The Philippines is a staunchly Roman Catholic enclave in Asia is apparent to everyone from the moment of arrival. But the traditional Christian festivals celebrating the agony and glory of Christ, have, over the four centuries since Magellan's arrival, blended with the native animism of the original tribes and the natural exuberance of the Filipino character to coalesce into a unique religious happening.

The names are the same — Christmas, Easter, etc., — but the actual celebrations themselves seem to have a different tone than the same holiday in the West. Take the sombreness of a Christian holiday, add a bit of pagan ritual, Spanish fiesta, mix well with sword or cross, and sprinkle liberally with Filipino gaiety and humour — and you have a "Christian" holiday, Philippine style.

The more sombre sanctity of the Vatican seems to have been lost in transit over the years, for whilst Christ is at the very centre of virtually all Filipino life and every fiesta, the surrounding pageantry and trappings are a bizarre blend of faith and frenzy, catechism and carousal. Filipino fiestas have as much solemnity as the annual *Mardi Gras* in New Orleans or Rio de Janeiro. It is hard to tell at times whether the festivals in the country are pagan with a Christian overlay or *vice versa*. And at this stage in Filipino history, the exact origins probably do not matter to the average visitor who is more interested in a superb show.

Over the centuries of Spanish influence, for example, the paganistic mysticism of the *shaman* (the medicine man or chief with supernatural powers) was cunningly transferred to the statue of

the Christ Child (and later to the images of the Virgin Mary) by the clever Spanish padres, who in turn became the masters of the "magic spell." **Sto. Nino** became the first of the "miracle" Christian icons, of which there are about 50 of the Christ Child and the Virgin Mary throughout the country. Sto. Nino processions and celebrations take place over the entire archipelago during the fiesta of Sto. Nino on the third weekend of January. At this time, many of the Sto. Ninos in private collections are gathered for a grand parade which winds its way through the cities' streets to the main cathedrals or churches to be blessed. In Manila, the procession is usually about two miles long and takes about two to three hours to pass one point.

Though the image of the Christ Child started everything, the most spectacular of the Christian celebrations is during Holy Week.

The island of **Marinduque**, 580 kilometres south of Manila, becomes the focal point for one of the most bizarre Easter fiestas in the country, the **Moriones Festival**. Here, the cult of Christ has become an incredible mixture of Christian history, fantasy, ancient animism and of course local mythology. The main celebrations take place in the capital **Boac**, with equally fervent

celebrations in **Gasan** and **Mogpog**.

This event, a unique mixture of faith and carnival frenzy, re-enacts the tale of Longinus, a Roman centurion who was blind in one eye and was the centurion who pierced Christ's left side with a lance so that he might die without prolonged agony. A drop of blood spattered into his blind eye and his sight was miraculously restored. When Longinus then witnessed Christ's resurrection while guarding the closed tomb, he converted immediately to Christianity and began preaching the message of God. This didn't go down too well with the Roman authorities, who sent legionnaires to pursue and apprehend him. He was eventually brought to trial before the infamous Pontius Pilate, sentenced to death and beheaded.

The festival kicks off with the *kalbaryuhan* (Calvary), traditional Filipino passion plays in *Tagalog* which re-enact the crucifixion. "Christ" is led out of Boac's church fortress on the morning of Good Friday and is taken to a hill where he is crucified, with Longinus' assistance, at 3pm Good Friday. Flagellants now take over the pageant. Mostly men, they whip their bare backs into a bloody mess. Saturday is usually a quiet day, building up to the *pugutan* (beheading) of Longinus on Sunday.

The Moriones festival begins on Holy Wednesday and from that moment until its climax on Easter Sunday its participants, called *Morions* (which means "plumed helmet" in Spanish) wander the streets of Marinduque dressed as Roman centurions, girded with swords of tin or wood and wearing bizarre carved masks (*dapdap*) of Indian coral wood with sharp painted noses, fierce, penetrating eyes and beards or moustaches. The costumes, incidentally, are usually home-made.

Opposite, *students struggle for the honour of pulling the rope to haul the statue of the Black Nazarene in Quiapo, Manila.* Centre, *all decked out in his festival finery, this participant in the Ati-Atihan festival has readied himself for the three-day celebration.*

Like some conquering force settling back for a bit of Bacchanalia, the centurions flirt with the ladies, serenade the shopkeepers and frighten the children, beating together two wooden sticks called *kalutang* which they carry with them. Each day there are parades, with local brass bands thumping out music ranging from hymns to New Orleans jazz.

The main spectacle of the festival takes place on Easter Sunday when the Morions and thousands of spectators — many of them also dressed as legionnaires — pack into an enormous open-air arena alongside the Boac River. With great theatricality, Christ's resurrection is re-enacted.

The wrath of the Roman legion is immediately aroused. the legionnaires are ordered to chase after Longinus and bring him to trial. He's pursued, caught and hauled before Pontius Pilate. Amid a great upswell of emotion, Longinus is beheaded. His "body" is placed on a bamboo litter and paraded through the town to the fortress cathedral of Boac.

Nowhere in The Philippines is there such a spectacular religious show as the Moriones Festival, but there *are* others almost as exciting. For example, in the small *barrio* (village) of **San Pedro** in Pampanga province, 50 kilometres north of

Manila, a re-enactment of the crucifixion takes place at noon each Good Friday, with a march through the village to "Calvary" by the would-be "Christs" and a host of flagellants. In the town of **Orani** in Bataan province, a "traditional" crucifixion also takes place on Good Friday. At both of these rather gruesome pageants the would-be "Christs" are actually nailed to the cross with sterilised nails and painfully left there bleeding for a short while, the practice and the pain actually an expression of penitence.

Holy Week in Manila, as well as most other parts of the country, is a softer, less spectacular affair (though you can find flagellants just about anywhere if you look hard enough) in which traditional Christian piety replaces pain and the other passionate and more aesthetic nature of the Filipino shines through.

On Palm Sunday, on the exact hour at which Jesus entered Jerusalem,

thousands of people literally mob the Quiapo Church at the **Plaza Miranda**, waving masses of plaited palm fronds and fighting to catch a drop or two of holy water sprinkled from the church steps by officiating priests.

From Holy Monday until Good Friday, villages and towns throughout the entire archipelago stage the *Cenaculo*, which is a distinctly Filipino version of the Passion Play. What makes these dramatic, highly stylised four-hour performances peculiarly Filipino is that musical accompaniment is usually provided by a local brass band, the script wanders right off the subject of Christ and includes matters like the Creation, the banishment of Adam and Eve from Paradise and the killing of Abel, the audiences eat and drink and chatter freely amongst themselves right through the plays and the more festive spectators often clamber up on to the stage and try to compete with the actors.

On Holy Saturday a calm descends upon the Easter ritual. The nation waits, and this quiet atmosphere of anticipation lasts throughout the day and well into the evening. It's not until midnight or thereabouts that prayers begin again in the churches, with priests conducting the Lighting of the Paschal Candles and the Blessing of the Baptismal Waters.

The Churches are in total darkness — the only source of light coming from burning coals in the outer courtyards. This symbolises the darkness of sin that enveloped mankind when Christ died upon the cross. Darkness is suddenly, dramatically banished during the *Gloria* of the Mass, when all the bells ring out, the organ bursts into tune and sacred images which until now have been veiled are uncovered. The priest lights the Paschal Candle and, one by one, the huge congregation touch their own candles to it. The churches gradually become ablaze with light. Christ has arisen.

A less religious but more colourful fiesta is the riotous *Ati-Atihan*, held in the third week of January in **Kalibo** on the island of Panay. Here, the cult of Christ is again at the centre of the festival's theme, but this time it is so overshadowed by fancy dress, dancing and merrymaking that the feast has actually been compared with the Mardis Gras of New Orleans and Rio de Janiero, but it has none of the pre-Lenten overtones.

Ati-Atihan, is a three-day folk festival which celebrates the harvest and also Sto. Nino, the patron saint of Kalibo.

The festival commemorates the arrival of four *datus* (chiefs) driven out of their home in Borneo in 1212. In a deal reminiscent of the purchase of Manhattan Island from the Indians, the wily *datus* purchased Panay from King Marikduo, the leader of the *Atis* (or *Aeta*), the original occupants — the black kinky-

---

Holy Week in the Philippines is celebrated with pageants, some of which feature actual crucifixions, and Filipino versions of Passion Plays.

25

haired, pygmy-like aboriginals (also called Negritos) — for a golden *salakot* (the special headgear worn by the natives) and a golden necklace for Queen Maniwangtiwang. Naturally the *datus* celebrated the sale and for a bit of fun, they dabbed themselves with soot to receive their Negrito guests. Presumably the Negritos were not offended. Catholicism gets into the act because Christian-Malays were once saved from plunder by a Muslim pirate by the appearance of Sto. Nino. So, the Filipinos have combined a friendship ceremony, a harvest celebration and a religious miracle into one super bash.

Picture a Filipino, covered head-to-toe in soot, hair stiffened and standing straight, dressed in the bib'n tuck of a 13th century aboriginal, swigging out of a container of *tuba* (fermented coconut juice which is highly potent) from one hand and clutching a jewelled icon of Sto. Nino with the other, and you have a good idea of what Ati-Atihan is all about.

Multiply the image by thousands, add dozens of brass bands and several parades, and you have a fair idea of the magnificent chaos which takes place over the weekend.

The people of Panay's *barrios* (villages) form themselves into different "Ati tribes," each of which conjures up a different theme or design for their costumes. The materials they use are cheap and easily obtained — sea-shells, papier mâché, coconuts, straw, palm fronds — but the results are incredibly striking; when the "tribes" take to the streets in a mass of dancing, drumming, singing war-parties, the burst of colour and ingenuity is such that one can only imagine a mammoth pagan spectacle directed by the immortal Cecil B. de Mille.

Every day, from dawn to dusk, thousands of "warriors" and spectators prance, jiggle, shimmy and stomp their way through the streets to the town square. Amid the cacaphony, almost as an afterthought, one can hear an occasional yell of "Viva El Senor, Sto.

Nino!" (Long Live the Holy Child Jesus!)

The Christian aspect of the great festival breaks through the revelry on the last day, Sunday. After mass in the local **Church of the Santo Nino**, a vast four-hour procession made up of some 50 or more "tribes" hits the streets, accompanied by gaily decorated floats, and Ati-Atihan climaxes in a long, deafening thunder of drums. Followed by yet another night of carousing.

Though the Ati-Atihan Fiesta in Kalibo is the most famous in the Philippines, there are various Ati-Atihan festivals throughout the country, including Cadiz City, Cubao, Quezon City, Manila's Tondo section; even at the Tropical Paradise Resort Hotel in Manila.

Christmas season in the Philippines begins on December 16th, with the *Misa de Gallo* (Rooster's Mass) and ends on January 6th with the celebration of the Three Kings. Each region has its own variation on the traditional Christmas theme. Carolling to some may recall images of Irving Berlin's *White Christmas*, complete with Bing Crosby's dulcet tones, and children bundled up against the snow, but in the Bicol region of Southern Luzon, carollers dress as *pastores* (shepherds) while in Cebu they have dyed or smudged faces and come out looking like Ati-Atihan celebrants. In the Western Visayas, the carollers (called *daigons*) not only serenade, but dance and perform comedy skits.

Once December 16 is past, the Christmas atmosphere sprouts at home. Trees are trimmed while *belen*, the familiar nativity scene springs up in every lawn or garden or plaza. Incidentally, the domestic animals of the manger scene include *carabao* (water buffalo) which seems incongruous to many Westerners but not to the Filipinos.

Midnight Mass on Christmas Eve is of course a hallowed Christian tradition, but the Filipinos, in their own inimitable style, have added the **Misa de Aguinaldo** (Mass of Gifts). The traditional Christmas feast *Noche Buena*, is held after the *Misa de*

Aguinaldo, in the early hours of Christmas morning, and not on mid-Christmas Day; Santa Claus, to a young Filipino child is his *Ninong* (godfather) and *Ninang* (godmother). In true Filipino style, each child has two sets, one for baptism and one for confirmation.

The entire country is lit up during this time from the smallest home in a remote *barrio* to the vast Plaza Miranda in Manila. Homes and churches and public buildings are awash with light. Incidentally, Merry Christmas is *Maligayang Pasko*!

Parols (lanterns) play a great part in the decoration and in the town of San Fernando, in the central Philippines province of Pampanga, the largest and most spectacular Lantern Festival in the country is held. Lanterns, some as large as 5-10 metres in diameter with hundreds of lights, bathe the town in a kaleidoscope of colours.

New Year's Eve of course explodes into revelry — fireworks and balls, general merrymaking not unlike the partying found all over the Western world. But New Year's Day, is *Pasko ng mga Dalaga at Binata* (Christmas of the Lovers) during which sweethearts go to mass together and exchange gifts.

If you are in Manila on January 9, that is the day of the Feast of the Black Nazarene in the old Quiapo Church in the Manila *arrabales* (district) of the same name. It is the first, and probably the most unique of the Sto. Nino celebrations.

On the stroke of two in the afternoon, a huge black statue of Jesus seated on a solid pedestal is carried out of the church, followed by another *carroza* bearing a life-size image of the Virgin Mary. Thousands of teenagers with "Jesus Nazareno" printed on their T-shirts and white towels wrapped around their heads or shoulders rush forward and struggle for the honour of grabbing one of two ropes by which the Black Nazarene is dragged through the streets; while the women march sedately behind the Virgin clad in gowns of deep purple, wearing crowns of thorns and bearing candles and brightly coloured parasols. As the huge procession makes it way through the streets, thousands of onlookers try to touch the Black Nazarene with a towel or handkerchief, then symbolically cleanse themselves of all sins and ailments by rubbing their entire bodies with the sanctified cloths.

Youngsters scramble to get a look at a huge statue of Jesus which is carried through the streets in a procession.

It is possible to hit the Philippines in mid-December and never stop celebrating something until the end of January!

May 15 in the town of Pulilan in Bulacan is St. Isidro's Day, the patron saint. On that day, the farmers from the surrounding area bring their *carabao* to town for the annual Carabao Festival. Believe it or not, each and every animal has been freshly bathed and scrubbed, their toe nails manicured, their tails combed and adorned with garlands of flowers like so many Roman virgins. The *carabao*, no doubt unmindful of what is happening and dying to get back to a cool and delightful mudbath, are gathered in the church courtyard where the resident priest duly blesses them and sprinkles holy water over the herd. The main plaza of the town is then the site for

carabao races, later in the day. There are also Carabao Festivals in May in Pavia, Iloilo.

People are drenched on the streets in San Juan, Rizal on June 24, each year as the community commemorates the feast of St. John the baptist.

The Penafrancia Festival in Naga City, Camarines Sur, which takes place on the third weekend of September, is one of the most spectacular of the river festivals featuring fluvial parades. Other fluvial festivals include *Pista ng Krus* in June celebrating a bountiful harvest in Obando, Bulacan, the Feasts of Saints Peter and Paul on June 28-30 in Apalit, Pampanga, and the Bocaue River Festival in Bocaue, Bulacan on July 4-7.

Though the country is so overwhelmingly Roman Catholic that

long celebration of traditional dancing and feasting.

In July, in the Mountain Province of Northern Luzon, there's another Harvest Festival which gives the five major ethnic groups making up the Ifugao (the mountain people) a chance to show off their traditions. Baguio City, the capital of Benguet Province, also has a smaller festival during Holy Week which combines Easter celebrations with *Cañao* the tribal gathering of the Ifugaos.

The Kaamulan festival in Malaybalay, Bukidnon (Mindanao) provides opportunity for the eight tribal groups of this area to get together each October.

A Muslim festival of Hariraya Puasa is celebrated all over Mindanao in November, and marks the end of Ramadan, the month-long fasting period celebrated during the ninth month of the Muslim calender.

Visitors to the Philippines are exposed to more Muslim culture than they realise. Just about every "cultural show" put on by the various hotels and travel agencies in Manila, consists of some Muslim dancing, usually the famous "stick dance" where a Muslim princess in magnificent Muslim garb intricately steps her way through the clacking sticks with her hand-maiden, carrying the parasol, in attendance, and the suitor or prince deftly following.

One of the brochures on the Philippines claims there are about 1000 festivals annually — a little less than three a day — in the country. The official list, available from the tourist agencies lists only 86 and is admittedly not complete. If you attempt to "follow the fiestas" for a year you will not only have demonstrated a steel-like stamina, but you'll end up with a superb insight of the country and the people, one that very few Filipinos themselves even have.

just about any day of the year will find a Filipino-Christianised fiesta or fête somewhere in the country, there are sizeable ethnic minorities which quite naturally celebrate festivals of their own. The largest minority in the archipelago are the Muslims, who mostly live on the island of Mindanao and are divided into about 60 different groups.

Because of the continuing war there, many of these festivals — such as the colourful Yakan Harvest Festival on the island of Basilan held each November — cannot be attended. However, there are a few that are still accessible. The largest is the gathering of the tribes in Davao City in June. Most of the 21 tribes from that Eastern area of Mindanao, as far West as Cotobato and as far North as Cagayan d'Oro converge on the city for a week-

The Filipinos love for colour is expressed in their photogenic costumes. Here, a town fiesta in Ozamis City. Following pages, a fishermen's island in the Sulu Archipelago.

Pagan Peoples
Mountain Tribes and Other Minorities

Of the 47 million Filipinos, less than 10 percent, around four million, are designated "cultural minorities." More than half of the minorities are Muslims from Mindanao island and the Sulu Archipelago in the south. The remainder range from stone-age aboriginals deep in rain forests to peaceful yet dramatic mountain folk tilling their terraced lands as they have for centuries.

In 1967 the federal government created a foundation, PANAMIN (Presidential Assistance on National Minorities) whose chairman is a member of the Cabinet. The object of PANAMIN is to help and protect the minorities, most of whom are quite primitive and poor and many of whom are well out of the mainstream of Filipino life, and would otherwise — it is said — easily fall prey to some of the cultural and economic influences of the 20th century.

The newest group to come under PANAMIN's protection is the Tasaday, a stone-age tribe of just 27 people living deep in a rain forest in South Cotabato, Mindanao. "Civilisation" discovered them in 1971, though they had a few sporadic contacts with hunters from tribes on the edge of their rain forest. PANAMIN has wisely protected the Tasadays from the outside influences (like loggers and tourists) by limiting access to them and by protecting 20,000 hectares of rain forest as their preserve.

Interestingly, the Tasadays report at least two other tribes living even deeper in the forest, and attempts are being made to contact them.

Though the Tasadays are now the most famous of the primitive tribal minorities in The Philippines, there are many other tribes and groups more accessible, more civilised (literally), though just as fascinating in their own right.

The most popular are those from the mountainous area of northern Luzon, the reason being their easy accessibility. Travellers with little time to spare can make a swift one-hour trip by air to the summer capital of The Philippines, **Baguio**, which is the major tribal market-place for the area. There, it's possible to buy some of the traditional weavings and basket-ware from the mountain tribes, spot the occasional tattooed tribesman on his rare trip to town and return to Manila within 24 hours. For those with a bit more time and energy, it's possible to continue up into the mountains and spend time with the Igorots on their own turf.

Igorot is not a tribe, but rather a general term referring to all the mountain people of the rugged Cordillera mountain range. The term encompasses five major ethnic groupings: the Benguets, Bontocs, Ifugaos, Kalingas and Apayaos.

The Benguets are the first group travellers to Baguio come across since they live in the western and southern sections of the Cordillera. A peaceful people, they are noted farmers. A trip to Baguio's market place to inspect the myriad of produce available or a trip to the valley below Baguio about five km away and its capital **La Trinidad** will find them. A gathering of the Benguets for a community feast is called a *Canao*, and something not to be missed if it coincides with your visit.

The Ifugaos of the Central Cordillera area are famous for their rice terraces which the Filipinos, and outsiders, regard as the eighth wonder of the world. The central point of this area is the town of **Banawe**, nestled in the mountains at the 1,500-metre level. The Ifugaos are also regarded as artisans and superb woodcarvers, not just of their gods and idols or handicrafts, but their stilted houses as well.

The Bontocs are also famous, but for another reason. They were once fierce warriors and headhunters. This deadly practice has, of course, been forbidden for many years, though heads were said to have been taken as late as the 1950's during the *huk* rebellion. The tattooing which adorns the Bontoc men used to symbolise manhood, attained of course by war and the taking of heads. (Other tribes — particularly the Ifugao, wear tattoos, but are not headhunters).

The Bontoc, particularly, were early targets of American Protestant missionaries in the early part of this century. Even now, in the depths of the mountain range, the fluency and high standard of English is quite surprising. In fact, the standard of English spoken in all the mountainous areas is high, a direct result of the missionaries — past and present.

The Kalingas live in the northeast section of the Cordillera range. More isolated because of their geography, they too were once headhunters. In fact, they still enter peace pacts with neighbouring tribes and are regarded as rather belligerent. They are quite hospitable to visitors though. During their gatherings, their tradition of story-telling comes to the fore, along with a vast collection of tribal dances. The spiritual lubricant for all this entertaining is *basi*, a sugar cane wine with enough potency to grow hair on a billiard ball.

The Apayaos are the least studied tribe, probably because they are located in the northern most part of the mountain range. They still hunt with the bow and arrow, wear tattoos and, like the Kalingas, have a good reputation for hospitality.

Another tribal grouping in the area, the Tingguisans, are a minority within the five main tribes. They are descendants of the early Polynesians who settled in northern Luzon. They dwell in the high mountain valleys and are known for their super weaving. Because of their juxtaposition between the highland tribes and the lowlanders of the adjacent provinces, they seem to have absorbed some of both cultures.

Though the American missionaries made strong attempts to Christianise the mountain tribes, and to a degree succeeded where the Spanish *padres*

(backed by their conquistadores) failed, the tribes are still a very animistic and polytheistic people. Christians naturally enough regarded them as pagans, and still do, no doubt. Their burial practices are one of the major attractions these days. The burial caves and 500-year-old mummies of the Igorots in Mount Timbac in the Kabayan area and the village of Sagada about 15 km west of Bontoc in the Mountain Province are still major attractions for the mountain people and visitors alike.

Most minorities are poor compared to other Filipinos and receive assitance from the government. Opposite, *a shy girl from the* Umayamnon *tribe in Bukidnon Province.* Above, *dressed in their holiday best, women of the* Talaandig *tribe at the Kaamulan Festival held each year in Bukidnon.*

Another group inhabiting this area are the Negritos, negroid aborigines of many different tribes numbering about 40,000. Though mostly found in this area, Negritos are also found in the jungles of Leyte, Samar Negros and Palawan. The Negritos are a kinky-haired, dark race, very small in stature — almost pygmies — and quite obviously descended from a very different people than the proto-Malays normally associated with the heritage of the average Filipinos. Many of the Negrito tribes still live deep in forests, though they are not "lost" to the 20th century Philippines because they do have frequent trading contacts. They are superb hunters, with their bows and arrows and spears, and still manage to live off the land. They live in lean-to type structures and lead very isolated lives. There is no apparent cultural unity between the various Negrito tribes. Their clothing is usually limited to bark cloth and, though hunters, they also till the land, moving on to another site when dissatisfied. Some of the most isolated of these Negrito tribes are found deep in the forests of Isabella province in northern Luzon.

One such remote tribe is the Pugots, who "though they speak Kalinga" (after the main tribe of the area), are distinct from them. They live deep in a forest in northern Isabella Province, only occasionally venturing into neighbouring *barrios* (villages) to trade game for some of civilisation's goodies.

There is also a very primitive Negrito tribe, the Batak, deep in the forests of Palawan Island. They are quite timid, afraid of the civilisation which is spreading fast on Palawan as the island develops into the country's oil centre, and are said to adorn themselves with flowers.

The Muslim tribes in the south are also referred to as Moros. Their ancestors were here before the Spanish and regard themselves as quite independent of not only the Manila government, but of each other. There are more than 60 tribes in Mindanao and they are the largest minority group in the country. The on-

going war against the central government in Manila aims for complete independence of the Muslim south. The Moros fall into five major groupings: the Tausug, Maranao, Maguindanao, Samal and the Badjao.

The Tausug (which means "people of the current") were the first to be converted to Islam and ruled the area from the island of Jolo. They consider themselves to be superior and purer than the other Muslim tribes because of their historical antecendents. As a group they are regarded as pugnacious in almost a *macho* sense — personal combat being not only part of life, but a constant test of life.

Juxtaposed with their agressiveness is an artistry. They are artisans of both excellent weapons and beautiful cloth. They are fishing folk too, which also means they are traditionally traders and smugglers, and the barter markets of Zamboanga are their domain.

The Samals live and die by the sea in villages built on stilts over the sea. Traditionally, the Samal from Sulu are the weavers of the striking *pandan* mats. However they have suffered greatly from the brief war which all but destroyed the capital, Jolo.

The Philippines' minorities reflect a wide variety of cultural influences. Opposite, *a girl of the* Yakan *tribe in the island of Basilan in southern Mindanao.* Above, *an* Ilongot *father and son in Isabela Province, north of Luzon.*

The last group, the Badjao, are true boat-people — sea gypies. They sail the waters of the Sulu Archipelago and the coastal waters of Mindanao, literally living and dying on their flimsy *vintas* (outrigger sailing canoes). They make their living these days through subsistence fishing, diving for coral and shells and selling some. The smallest Moro group, numbering only about 25,000, they are not as fervent Muslims as their neighbours, the Samal, with whom they are supposed to be related.

Southwestern Mindanao is the home of the Tiruray tribe. They are one of the

abundant.

On the east side of the Gulf of Davao live the Bagobos. They are weavers too, mostly of cloth from abaca. They decorate weapons in the Moro tradition, but they themselves are not warriors.

In Bukidnon in East Lanao, there are eight different groupings under the Bukidnon, totalling no more than 50,000. They are a fiercely independent tribe but live in relative peace with seven other tribes (Ilianon, Matigsalug, Pulangiyon, Tigwahanon, Talaandig, Umayamnon and Manobo) in the area.

The list goes on. In Western Lanao is a tribe called the Subanon who live by the rivers and produce the best pottery.

The sad thing about most of these tribes is that they are off-limits to foreigners. The areas are not necessarily inaccessible, nor the tribes so primitive that permission from PANAMIN is needed. It is just that the long war between the Philippine Government and the Moro National Liberation Front has spilled over virtually the entire island and throughout the Sulu archipelago and foreigners are just not allowed into most of the interesting areas because of the unrest. Until the fighting ends and peace is restored the mountain tribes of the northern Philippines will remain the most popular pagan peoples on the tourist trek.

unique tribal minorities. They live communally, practising polygamy. They are a Malay people who for some reason have developed as skilled horsemen, a skill unique among the tribes of The Philippines.

The Lake Cibu area in Cotabo is the home of the T'boli tribe, which has had much contact with the outside world. Their music and dancing is the showpiece of many "cultural" shows seen in Manila. They too are skilled designers and weavers and have even created their own type of hemp or cloth called *t'nalak*. Their brassware is also well known and

Dress among the minorities ranges from elaborately beaded and embroidered creations to "bare" basic. Opposite, daily dress of the Manobo tribe. Centre, above, Palawanan tribespeople. Following pages, a family of Tagbanua tribespeople in Palawan, west of Quezon.

The Tourist Trail
On the Beaten Track

Metro Manila

Many visitors, winging into the Philippine capital, Manila, for the first time, have described it as urbanisation in a state of anarchy. To some extent it is: Manila is made up of some 17 separate, distinct and independent municipalities — four cities and 13 towns, in fact — spread over something like 635 square kilometres. Manila didn't just happen, it kind of *spread*, with scarcely any planning and very little integration and cooperation between the various citadels of municipal power.

Yet the spirit of that anarchy is, to a great extent, part of the city's rather dramatic charm — for it reflects the freewheeling, happy-go-lucky spirit of the Filipinos themselves. But it is an indestructible spirit, in the face of two latter-day campaigns to bring the urban and individual anarchy under control:

The martial law brought in by President Ferdinand E. Marcos and the governorship of Manila by his First Lady, Imelda, which has at least brought the city's 17 communities under one authority.

Manila is a man-made maelstrom of wide, multi-laned boulevards and highways cutting across or circling thousands of narrow, crowded pot-holed, traffic-choked, fume-enshrouded streets, zig-zagging off the main thoroughfares at every angle. Taxi drivers know their way through this back-street maze to virtually every corner of the city, of course, so an average journey from, say, the luxury hotels or commercial centres of **Makati**, or the **Manila International Airport** beyond (or vice versa), will include combinations of wide avenues and disturbingly narrow and rustic back lanes as the taxi jostles for room, the driver switching back and forth between his horn and accelerator, until, with a final bellow of the horn, he bursts out on to the lovely tree-lined **Roxas Boulevard**, which runs along the shore of **Manila Bay**. The dead, stifling heat of the narrow lanes, where hardly a breath of cool air stirs, except during typhoons, gives way to cool sea breezes and the baking heat of the sun beating down on the boulevard's long miles of black asphalt. Roxas Boulevard is one tremendously long rank of hotels and restaurants, clubs and massage parlours — but it's so long that few of the big buildings are jammed together until you get toward the town centre.

Intramuros

Like most old cities — and "modern" Manila dates from 1571 — the urban metropolis of today has blossomed from the tiny kernel of the original ancient township. The kernel was **Intramuros** (which means "within these walls"). Located on the south bank of the **Pasig River**, which bisects the city now as it did in the 16th century, Intramuros is the magnet for virtually all organised or individual tours in the city.

More than just one of the finest examples of medieval European architecture this side of Suez, Intramuros is a remnant and living museum piece of the citadel of Spanish power which did so much to shape the culture of The Philippines.

Unlike other former colonies, The Philippines seems proud of this cultural umbilical cord to its Spanish past. The country has not destroyed or hidden or denied its Spanish heritage. On the contrary, it has preserved it.

The first Spanish forts on the original city site were of spiked bamboo logs. The actual construction of the massive stone walls, rising three metres tall and 13 meters thick in some places, was started in 1590. The perimeter of the walls was about three miles, enclosing an enclave of narrow well planned streets, modest plazas, a dozen churches and a fort. The

moat was added in 1603 and access to the city was by drawbridge until the 19th century, when a series of earthquakes caused the Spanish authorities to seal the gates. The moat was filled in during the American administration of this century because it was deemed a "health hazard."

Today, Intramuros is included in virtually all the organised city tours, but to enjoy the historic place and capture its real historic flavour you'd be well advised to go alone, leave a bit of time to wander through the streets which are peaceful, stunningly silent when compared with the beeping, smoky chaos on most of Manila's overcrowded streets and avenues.

Of the dozen churches, once places of worship for Spanish nobles with the confines of Intramuros, only two remain: **San Agustin**, the oldest church in The Philippines, and the **Manila Cathedral**. Most Filipinos consider it an "act of God" that San Agustin is still intact and functioning. It survived the earthquakes of 1645, 1754, 1852, 1863 and 1880, which caused much damage to the city

— and the bombings of World War II and the last stand by the Japanese occupation forces, which reduced much of Intramuros to rubble. Restoration of the walled city was begun in 1978. The church today houses the ashes of some of the famous *conquistadores*, including Legazpi's. On the ground floor of the original monastery is a museum.

The Manila Cathedral is, in fact, the fifth cathedral of that name on that location. The first nipa palm structure was burnt in 1574. The next two were also destroyed by fire, (while San Agustin, just a short distance away, was spared). The fourth, built between 1870 and 1879, probably would have survived if it had not been bombed in World War II (and San Agustin, just a short distance away, was spared again). The present cathedral dates from 1954 and was dedicated in 1958.

Fort Santiago

Intramuros also houses **Fort Santiago**, the defensive lynchpin of the Spanish

realm. It was constructed over a 149-year period and completed in 1872. The history of Fort Santiago shows not only the grandeur of the Spanish empire, but the cruelties that the Spanish were capable of. The dungeons flooded with water from the **Pasig River** at high tide and countless *indios* (native Filipinos) met a watery death in them. The Spanish carried out many of their executions in Fort Santiago, though one of the most famous, that of Dr. José Rizal in 1896 which sparked off the revolution which ended the Spanish rule, was actually carried out in (what is now) Rizal Park (La Luneta). However, Rizal spent his last hours in the dungeons of Fort Santiago.

After the Americans took The Philippines from Spain in 1898, the seat of government was moved to the **Malacanang Palace**, which is now the official home of the president of The Philippines and another striking cultural attraction of Fort Santiago. The Fort is now a lovely park area and a favourite rendezvous for promenaders. It also houses the **Rizal Museum** dedicated, as the name implies, to the founding hero of the republic; the **Rajah Sulayman** (open air) **Theatre** (in the former barracks) where Filipino repertory theatres perform new and traditional plays; and a

Centre, *A "Concert in the Park" is held every Sunday at the Luneta Park.* Above, *thousands fill the Plaza Miranda in Manila for the Quiapo Fiesta.*

45

collection of old cars, formerly driven by Filipino presidents, and an old woodburning steam engine (used by General Luna as his headquarters during the 1898 Filipino-American war), underneath the western ramparts.

La Luneta

Rizal Memorial Park — also known as La Luneta (little moon) for its shape — separates Intramuros and **Ermita**, one of the main tourist shopping and entertainment sections of the city. The park houses another memorial to Dr. Rizal and his exact execution spot is marked. But the park covers a vast area, divided into many sections. The **Quirino bandstand** is the site of regular official ceremonies, and *tai chi* (Chinese shadow boxing) exercises during the early morning hours — as well as open air concerts. There are also two beautiful traditional gardens, one Chinese and one Japanese, in addition to a children's playground where the kiddies frolic over pre-historic stone monsters decorated in garish colours. The park also houses the **National Library**, the **Planetarium**, and the **Aquarium**, as well as a 17-hole **Municipal Golf Course**.

Chinatown

Chinatown, which straddles the **Binondo** and **Tondo** sections, is another part of Manila worth seeing. Cross over the Pasig River via the **Jones Bridge** and go through the **Arch of Goodwill**, and there you are. The settlement dates from 1594 when the Chinese traders within Intramuros were burned out and relocated outside the walls in the **Parian** (silkmarket) area. The Chinese were referred to by the Spanish as *Sangkeys*, from the Amoy word *seng-li* (trade). **Escolta Street**, the main street of Chinatown, is small and it is hard to believe it was the main commercial avenue of the city. The street still has a 19th century colonial air about it. Naturally, Chinatown is the site of

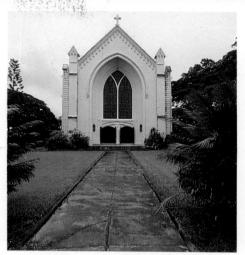

Chinese restaurants, herbalists, temples, shops, markets, *godowns* (warehouses), *mahjong* parlours, kung fu schools, acupuncture clinics, tea houses, all existing cheek-by-jowl along the crowded and bustling thoroughfares, some of which are still cobbled, and have incongruous Spanish names.

Arranque Market (walk down **Alonzo Street**, an interesting restaurant street in its own right) is the area's main shopping mecca and, being Chinese, offers different items from the other city markets.

It is in Chinatown that other remnants of the past congregate, namely the *calesas* and the *carretalas* (horse-drawn rigs), some with the original brass lamps on either side, which once were the main means of transportation in the city. (The intersection of **Ongpin** and **Alonzo Streets** is one main gathering point.) The "main street" of Chinatown is Ongpin Street where the crowds waiting to eat in the many restaurants literally spill out on to the pavements. Ongpin Street also has most of the jewellery shops. On **C.M. Recto Avenue** is a towering Buddhist pagoda watching over the din and hustle of daily commerce. The **Santo Seng Kong Church**, on **Morga Street**, which is off

The Church figures prominently in the lives of the people, whether it be a procession of the Knights of Columbus at the Sta. Cruz Church in Manila (opposite) or an austere chapel on the campus of Silliman University (above).

Juan Luna, the Tondo's main thoroughfare, has its own Sto. Nino, and — would you believe — 24 other icons from the major and minor religions of the world. The church's minister doubles as a geomancer (*fung shui* man) and the church itself is said to have been constructed on the advice "of a spiritual advisor from the planet Saturn."

The **Tondo** section, incidentally, is the most densely populated section of the capital, parts of which are squalid slums. It has been earmarked for redevelopment. Located along the Pasig River, it is the scene of a fluvial procession honouring Sto. Nino on the third Sunday of each January. The main railway station, **Tutuban,** is located in the Tondo. On the edge of this district is the **Divisoria Market,** a vast complex with some of the best buys available.

In **Binondo,** the other side of Chinatown, is the **Binondo Church** which originated in 1596. It was built by the Dominicans and the present church is a post-war reconstruction.

The Black Nazarene

Quiapo is another of the old sections of Manila worth visiting. The focal point here is the **Quiapo Church** with its Black Nazarene and the vast **Plaza Miranda**. January 9 is the *fiesta* day for Quiapo when the Black Nazarene (a full sized figure of Christ, kneeling, carrying the cross) is carried forth. Every Friday, the devotees hobble to the altar on their knees. On the Church patio are the traditional herb sellers, and organic cures, natural concoctions and amulets are all on sale to those with ailments. The cacophony of the hawkers' cries mixes with those of vendors selling commonplace items like balloons or sweepstake tickets and, of course, flowers. Just where **Evangelista** and **Carriedo Streets** converge are you'll find traditional palm readers.

Centrepoints

The **Ermita** section of Manila is well known to most tourists because of **M.H. del Pilar** and **A. Mabini Streets**, the two main shopping and entertainment areas. Hundreds of stores, restaurants, bars, *pensiones* huddle side-by-side for a couple of miles on these two parallel one-way streets, which are always jammed with jeepneys.

You'll find that the **Makati** area of Manila, though not really a "sightseeing" area, is visited quite often because it is the new business hub of the country, as well as a site for many well-to-do residential enclaves, and three or four new first-class hotels which have sprung up there in the past few years. All of a sudden, Makati is actually creating new roads to take care of the commercial demand.

The focal point of Makati is the Makati Commercial Centre, a mammoth shopping complex which not only houses hundreds of small shops, several large department stores and the **Intercontinental Hotel**, but also a couple of cinemas and dozens of bars and restaurants. It is a gigantic complex of air-conditioned buildings offering just

about everything under the sun. Great shopping, expecially if it's raining.

Historic Churches

Like many cities in Europe, the history of Manila can be traced through its churches, and historical places of worship are literally scattered throughout the city.

The **Malate Church**, in the district of the same name, straddles the shopping and entertainment streets of **M.H. del Pilar** and **A. Mabini**. For those who do not have much time for viewing historical churches, its location is ideal. The first church on the site was built toward the end of the 16th century. In 1762, the church was occupied by British forces who used it as a base to attack Intramuros. This church was destroyed in 1773 and the present edifice dates back to restoration around that time.

Las Pinas Church, located about 45 minutes away by car, is famous for its giant bamboo organ. Las Pinas dates from 1792 and was completed in 1819. Construction of the amazing bamboo organ was started in 1816 by Father Diego Ceva, and the reed stops were installed by 1824. Then, in 1850 the church and organ were damaged in an earthquake. The organ was dismantled and stored, and then damaged again when the building it was stored in suffered typhoon damage. And there the

Historical churches, such as this one, are scattered throughout the country. Here, *the Sarrat Church in Sarrat, Ilocos Norte.*

organ remained, lost to history, until it was rediscovered in 1911. In the meantime, the church was rebuilt in 1888. Over the next five decades, work progressed sporadically on the organ and in 1932 electric power was installed. (Originally it was powered by a windmill!) In 1973, the entire organ was shipped to Germany for restoration and was reinstalled in Las Pinas in 1975. The organ is now played regularly and is probably the only one in the world. Four metres wide, it has 174 bamboo pipes and 122 horizontal reeds of soft metal, a five-octave keyboard and 22 stops arranged vertically. One tube, the *pajaritas*, is designed so that when it is filled with water, the sound that ripples forth is like that of delicate bird-song.

The **Santa Ana Church** is famous for its excavations. The church itself was founded in 1578 by Fransiscan Fathers. This edifice and the convent date from 1720 after the first structure succumbed to an earthquake. The excavations are enclosed in a building but the walls are of glass. In 1961 archaeological excavations were begun on an unnatural mound adjacent the church, and ultimately 200 skeletons, judged to be 800 years old, and 1,500 pieces of pottery were discovered. The small museum in the church has a display of many of the relics.

Other major churches in the Metro-Manila area are:

Church of our Lady of Perpetual Help — A Romanesque church founded by Redemptorist Fathers in 1931. Destroyed in World War II and rebuilt in 1950. The Wednesday novena service is packed with devotees from all over the city area, more than those who flock to it on Sundays for mass. It's located in the **Baclaran** area of **Paranaque**.

Quadalupe Church Ruins — The ruins date form 1601 and are Augustinian. Surviving earthquakes, the place of worship was occupied and sacked by the British in 1762. Then it was damaged in an earthquake in 1880, repaired in 1882 and used as an orphanage and a trade school. It was destroyed in the Filipino-American war of 1898, and then restored. **Bernardino Street** at **Guadalupe Bridge**.

San Sebastian Church — Built in 1891 as, not surprisingly, an earthquake-proof church by the Recollect Fathers, who went to Belgium for the pre-fabricated steel parts. It's located in **Quiapo**.

"Philippine Village"

Nayong Pilipino (which means "Philippine Village" in *Tagalog*) is The Philippines in miniature set on a 35 hectare (86 acre) complex by the Manila International Airport, and is perfect for those who would like to see more of the archipelago, but have only a few days in-country and are confined to Manila. Six Philippine regions are represented at the village: Tagalog, Bicol, Cebu, Mindanao, Mountain Province and Vigan. Each region has a *barrio* (village) in the style of the "home" area, where you can also buy the local arts and crafts and other products. Many of the famous sites of The Philippines are reproduced in miniature. For example, the **Mayon Volcano**, the **Chocolate Hills**, the **Banaue Rice Terraces**, even Spanish houses from **Vigan** and a mosque from **Mindanao**. Sites in the village are connected by a free jeepney service.

National Museum

One rarely thinks of Manila as a museum town, but it is. The **National Museum** concentrates on archeology, anthropology and natural history and has a celebrated pre-historic skull segment from the **Tabon Cave** (*circa* 24,000 BC) and burial jars from the same diggings on **Palawan Island**. There is also a **Museum of Philippine Costumes**, the **Museum of Filipino Life**, a numismatic museum, a seashell museum, the **Metropolitan** (art) **Museum** and a museum displaying the minority tribes in the country.

Jeepney Factory

The ubiquitous jeepney with it silver horses and mirrors, and individual hand-painted pop-religious panels, is virtually a symbol of The Philippines. The jeepney owes its birth to surplus jeeps, left over from the World War II, which were converted into passenger carrying vehicles. Though many of the jeepneys plying the roads look as though they have just survived World War II, they are in fact manufactured in the country, and the jeepney factories have become an off-beat tourist attraction, where visitors can watch the decorators work. The one most frequently visited is the **Sarao Jeepney Factory** and it is just beyond the village **Las Pinas**, so it can be included in the same trip to the church with the famous bamboo organ.

Attractions

Aquarium — Palacio Street. 8am-8pm daily. One peso, children half.

Aviary — (Ayala Museum) Makati Avenue, 9am-6pm daily except Monday. three pesos, children half.

Chinese Cemetery — F. Huertas Street, Santa Cruz. 8am-6pm daily. Free.

The Harbour

Manila Bay is of course, one of the city's most beautiful panoramas, and sunset photographs of the bay adorn most guidebooks on The Philippines. Most people notice the bay from their hotel rooms or from their taxi when hurrying along **Roxas Boulevard**. Few take the time to walk along the boulevard to really relish the full view. However, there are varous boat tours of the harbour available, and the boat trip to Corregidor Island (see page 72) at the bay's mouth also takes in the whole scene. An invitation to cruise the bay on someone's yacht, or just for drinks on a boat moored at **Manila Yacht Club**, is another excellent if rarer opportunity to see **Manila Bay** and the perspective of the city from the water.

A typical country store — Filipino-style — called a sari-sari *store by the natives — sells a little bit of everything.* Following pages, *twilight at Manila Bay.*

Cultural Centre of The Philippines, Roxas Boulevard. National Centre for Art, Music and Theatre. 9am-6pm daily. One peso. Variable programmes. Calendar of events issued each month. Ticket prices range from two pesos up. Call 57-39-61 for box office information and reservations. Box office open from 10am-1pm, 2-5pm daily.

Folk Arts Theatre — Roxas Boulevard. Open-air theatre. 9am-6pm daily. Free. Call 50-02-28 for programme and ticket information. Home of the Bayanihan Philippines Dance company, a famous cultural troupe.

Fort Santiago — Intramuros. 8am-10pm daily. One peso per car and 10¢ per person.

Jeepney Factory — (Sarao), Main Highway, Las Pinas, (further up the road from Las Pinas Church). 8am-5pm. Free.

Mabini Shrine — Nagtahan Bridge, Pandacan, Manila. 8am-5pm daily. Donations.

Malacanang Palace — On Pasig River, not far form Intramuros. Not open to public but tours can be arranged for organisations and groups. Telephone 47-96-61, ext. 773.

Nayong Pilipino — (Philippines in Miniature) — next to Manila International Airport. 9am-7pm Monday to Thursday, 9am-8pm Friday to Sunday. (Jeepneys stop running during lunch.) Three pesos.

Parks and Wildlife Centre — Quezon Boulevard Extension, Quezon City. 6am-9pm daily. Free.

Philippine International Convention Centre — Roxas Boulevard. 9am-4pm daily. Two pesos, children half; includes guided tour.

Planetarium — P. Burgos St., North Side Rizal Park. Hour-long shows. 10.30am-1.30pm and 3.30pm-6pm daily. Two pesos, children half.

Zoo and Botanical Gardens — M. Adriatico Street, Ermita. 7am-6pm daily.

Alto Doll Museum — 2,000 dolls in Filipino dress depicting the country's history. 49 Guevarra St., San Juan, Rizal, 9am-6pm daily. Admission one peso.

Ayala Museum — collection of artifacts from pre-Spanish time. Unique feature is the 63 three-dimensional dioramas depicting pre-historic scenes. Walk-in aviary. Makati Ave., Makati. 9am-6pm daily except-Monday. Admission three pesos, children half.

Carfel Seashell Museum — A private collection of seashells from Southeast Asia, 20,000 different varieties. 1786 A. Mabini St., Malate, 8am-5pm daily. Free.

Cultural Centre of the Philippines — Country's largest collection of Chinese and Siamese ceramics, all excavated from sites throughout The Philippines. Museum, Art Gallery and library. Roxas Blvd. 9am-6pm daily. Admission one peso.

Lopez Museum Memorial — Paintings of the Spanish colonial times. A choice collection of Filipiniana. 10 Lancaster St. Pasay City. 7.30am-4.30pm daily except Sundays and Mondays.

Luz Gallery — Contemporary Filipino art and sculpture, 448 E. de los Santos Ave., Makati. 9am-6pm daily except Mondays. Half day Sunday. Free.

Metropolitan Museum — Continually changing art exhibitions. Roxas Blvd. 9am-6pm daily except Monday. Half day Sunday. Free.

Money Museum — History of money from pre-Christian times. One of the most complete collections in the world. Central Bank, Roxas Blvd. 10am-5pm daily except Monday. Admission 50¢, children half.

Museum of Filipino Life (Museo ng Buhay Pilipine) — a 19th century Manila home on stilts by the sea. 784 Quirino Ave., Panranaque. 9am-6pm daily except Monday. Admission two pesos.

BIRTHPLACE
OF
JUAN LUNA Y NOVICIO

PATRIOT AND FOREMOST FILIPINO PAINTER.
BORN IN BADOC, ILOCOS NORTE, 23 OCTOBER
1857; SON OF JOAQUIN LUNA DE SAN PEDRO
AND LAUREANA NOVICIO. STUDIED IN THE ATE-
NEO MUNICIPAL, ESCUELA DE BELLAS ARTES
AND ESCUELA NAUTICA IN MANILA; BECAME A
LICENSED PILOT AT 17. PUPIL OF LORENZO
GUERRERO, NOTED FILIPINO PAINTER. WENT
TO SPAIN, 1877, STUDIED IN THE ACADEMIA
DE BELLAS ARTES DE SAN FERNANDO, MADRID.
PAINTED IN ROME HIS FIRST FAMOUS WORK,
"THE DEATH OF CLEOPATRA". WON GOLD MEDAL
FOR HIS SPOLIARIUM AT THE INTERNATIONAL
PAINTING EXPOSITION, 1884, IN MADRID.
WON OTHER MEDALS AND HONORS IN EUROPE.
AMONG HIS OTHER NOTABLE PAINTINGS WERE
"THE BATTLE OF LEPANTO", "THE BLOOD COM-
PACT", "PEOPLE AND KINGS". CO-WORKER OF
RIZAL, LOPEZ-JAENA, DEL PILAR AND OTHER
FILIPINO REFORMERS IN EUROPE; WAS IN THE
DIPLOMATIC SERVICE OF THE FIRST PHILIP-
PINE REPUBLIC. DIED IN HONGKONG, 7 DE-
CEMBER 1899.

Museum of Philippine Art — Changing exhibition of paintings, carvings, and sculpture. Roxas Blvd. 9am-6pm daily except Monday.

Museum of Philippine Costumes — Complete collection of Filipino dress, including a collection of the *ternos* (the traditional butterfly-sleeve dress) of the women. T.M. Kalaw St. 9am-9pm daily except Monday. Admission three pesos, children half.

Museum of Philippine Traditional

Cultures — Four Galleries depicting the lifestyle, art and artifacts of some of the 60 or more minority tribes under the protection of PANAMIN. On the grounds of Nayong Pilipino, near Manila International Airport, Mindanao Section. Entire complex open 9am-7pm, Monday to Thursday, and 9am-8pm Friday to Sunday. Admission three pesos (to entire complex).

Numerous museums exist for the history buff. Here, a plaque from the museum of Juan Luna in Ilocos Norte.

55

National Museum — Antiques, artifacts, natural history exhibits, relics, archeology depicting the history of the country. Dept. of Tourism Bldg., Agrifina Circle, Rizal Park. 8am-5pm daily.

University of Philippines Museum of Anthropology — The history of the country through the stone age. Diliman, northeast of Quezon City. Daily.

University of San Tomas Museum — One of the great collections of *santos* (small carved painted statues of religious figures and saints), ceramics, porcelain. Sampaloc district. Daily.

Shopping

The Philippines is still one of the cheapest places to shop in the Southeast Asian region. The variety of handcrafted goods available is extraordinary. But this is *not* the place to buy camera gear or hi-fi sets. It *is* the place to buy hand-embroidered shirts (*barong tagologs*) and dresses, wood carvings or furniture, macrame, shell items, *capiz* (shell lamps or knick-knacks), shoes, straw and rattanware, brassware, basketware, guitars, silver filigree and, of course, cigars.

Manila has everthing. You could probably find a sample of every item produced in the country in the capital, and you would almost certainly have the choice of buying that item in an air-conditioned shopping centre or an open-air market. Remember though that, if you are travelling throughout The Philippines, and are after certain items made in particular areas, price them in Manila to get an idea where to start; but before buying, check the prices in the area where they are made.

For example, silver filigree, certain types of basketware and wood carvings are cheaper in **Baguio** and in the Mountain Province north of the summer capital. Guitars are cheaper in **Cebu**, the country's guitar capital. Hand woven *malongs*, brassware, betalnut boxes and batik are cheaper in **Mindanao**. *Santos*, the carved wooden religious figures (once

found in every church in the country and now being replaced by plaster-cast *santos*), are cheaper in the provinces than in Manila.

A word about duty-free shopping: Most of the duty free shops are in Manila with one in Cebu City. But they are spreading. Unlike other countries, visitors to The Philippines are allowed to buy in Duty Free Shops for use *inside* the country during their stay; alcohol (two bottles), cigarettes (two cartons), perfume, toilet water, soap and one other miscellaneous item. These purchases do *not* affect any purchases you may make at the airport for your onward journey. You will need your passport and onward ticket and the latter is marked. Duty free shops in Manila are located at the **Manila International Airport, Makati Commercial Centre, Philippine Plaza Hotel, Manila Hotel, Hilton Hotel, Hyatt-Regency Hotel, the Philippines International Convention Centre** (only when a major convention is on) and in the **Segura Building**, Gorordo Avenue, Cebu City.

Browsers are welcome here, but you'll probably end up walking away with your hands full of bargains. Above, *handicrafts sold at the* Pistang Pilipino *in the centre of Manila's tourist belt.* Right, *the San Andres Fruit Market.*

Bargaining is a *de rigueur* practise in any of the markets or street stalls throughout the country. In larger department stores, the prices are usually fixed but there are frequent "discount" sales to stimulate business. In the smaller boutique stores, though they claim a fixed price, it is not rare for them to give a further discount if hustled.

Even if you are short of time in Manila, it is still possible to get away from your hotel arcade or the big air-conditioned shopping complexes and find a market selling Filipino items at cheaper prices.

If your hotel is on Roxas Boulevard or in Ermita, try the **Flea Market** and the **Pistang Pilipino** in Ermita. The Flea Market fronts Roxas Boulevard while the Pistang Pilipino is behind, between A. Mabini and M.H. del Pilar Streets. Both areas have several dozen small shops selling everything from macrame to rattan, tiny little inexpensive knick-knacks to very large and expensive items, along with embroidered clothing (*barong*

tagalog, women's dresses).

Stretching along the seaward side of Roxas Boulevard from the Convention Centre-Cultural Centre complex in the direction of the airport (away from the centre of town) are the hundred or so shops of the **Philippine Trade Exhibits**. There are some handicrafts shops in this long parade of buildings, but you have to sort through the heavy industry stores to find them.

A. Mabini and M.H. del Pilar Streets, two traffic clogged one-way streets running from Ermita to Malate, are meccas for many different handicrafts shops and hundreds of stores selling Filipino products. Since the stores are so jammed together, it would pay to compare prices of the more common items, like capiz jewelry, embroidered shirts (*barong tagalog*) or dresses, or placemats or wooden carvings or baskets. In the small stores, bargain as hard as you can. On A. Mabini is a department store called *Tessoro's* which has branches

in many hotel arcades and in the **Makati Commercial Centre**. This main store is the biggest, has the largest selection of products throughout its five floors, and is the cheapest of all the *Tessoro's* in Manila. It is good for one-stop shopping. No bargaining. Running in between Mabini and Pilar Streets is **Cortada Street,** which in fact is a rather small lane. This "street" houses about a dozen tiny shops specialising in traditional Muslim handicrafts from Mindanao.

Divisoria market in **San Nicholas** is spread over abour 20 blocks, but there are sections for just about every product you could possibly imagine. The **Quinta** market in **Quiapo** (under the Quezon city bridge) is very near the famous Quiapo Church. Rattanware, baskets, capiz, macrame, embroidery ... everything is found under this bridge in tiny stalls. You should be able to get things about half price, compared with tags in the tourist shops uptown. Just by the Quinta market on **Carlos Palanca Street,** are two shops, **Balikbayan Handicrafts,** — which has a large warehouse/factory out back — and **Nortom Handicrafts**. Both these shops are similar to the handicraft shops in the tourist districts, but they are larger and cheaper.

While in Quiapo, **Carriedo Street** is famous for its shoe stores while **Puyat Street** is the place the buy cassette tapes and records. A wander down **Avenida Rizal** through the street bazaars is also interesting.

Chinatown Bargains

In **Chinatown**, the colonial-style main street **Escolta** was *the* shopping street of Manila until it was superceded by the shopping mall and Manila spread further out into the suburbs. It is still a good place to find porcelain and some silverware and the **Oceanic Commercial** is a good place to start. On Ongpin Street you will find dozens of jewellery shops, and while you are in Chinatown you may as well have a peek at the **Anranque Market**.

"Shoe Town"

If shoes are your particular goal, and you've had no luck finding the right ones at the right price, go to the source, Marakina, known in Manila as "shoe town." It's about 45 minutes from Manila and there is not one shop in the district that does not sell shoes.

Shopping Complexes

Many people do not like wandering through markets, bartering with avid stall holders, especially if it is hot or raining or both. The American invention of the shopping mall has taken hold in The Philippines to a degree never imagined in the USA. The most famous of all the shopping complexes is the **Makati Commercial Centre**. Next to it is the Greenbelt Park Complex. Areas around Makati have sprouted even more shopping and commercial centres. There are the **Magallenes Commercial Centre, Greenhills Commercial Centre** and the **Araneta** Commercial Centre (incorporating the **Ali Mall**). In Malate there is the **Harrison Shopping Plaza,**

which is just next to the **Century-Park Sheraton Hotel** and behind the **Holiday Inn**. These vast shopping complexes have everything from department stores to off-course betting for *Jai-alai* to restaurants, tiny boutiques and cinemas — even amusement centres and supermarkets. And while at the Makati Commercial Centre, take a wander down **Pasay Road**, which has quite a few small shops and boutiques interspersed among its restaurants.

Cigars

The Philippines is famous for its cigars, which are available all over the country. Both *Alhambra* and *La Flor de la Isabella* cigars have factories which, in addition to hand-rolling cigars, make to order hand-carved wooden humidor boxes which make excellent gifts.

Food and Restaurants

Contrary to first impressions, hamburgers and hot dogs are definitely *not* the national foods of The Philippines.

Neither is **paella**. The gastronomic remnants of the two colonial powers still exist, and in the case of America, it is virtually overpowering, but the real Filipino cuisine is unique and has the advantage of being concocted with virtually all fresh ingredients daily. The islands are a "horn of plenty" when it comes to seafood or fruits or vegetables or poultry or pork products, upon which the native gastronomic treats are based.

For many visitors, the first and only exposure to native Filipino food is the luncheon buffet at their hotel, which invariably features some Filipino dishes. Good as it may be in such elegant surroundings, it is in the speciality restaurants outside the confines of the hotels that the Filipino cuisine excels.

The cuisine of The Philippines has evolved over the centuries from Malay and Chinese influences which filled out the country's history as well as its stomach. Filipino food is more of a natural and milder blend of the spiced dishes of Indonesia or the Malay peninsula. The staple food is rice and is served at every meal, including breakfast (the base of which is, more often than not, the leftovers from the previous night's dinner). Rice is also consumed — sometimes in the form of cakes — during the day's *meriendas*, the daily snack periods.

Being an archipelago, *fruits de mer*, as one would expect, play an important part in the Filipino diet. In Filipino restaurants, fish is rarely steamed (as in Chinese kitchens) or baked (as in Western restaurants). It is served raw (*kinilaw*), charcoal grilled (*inihaw*), grilled (*sinugbang*) or in soup (*sinigang*).

Kinilaw is raw fish marinated in vinegar with a host of spices and the juice of the *kalamansi* (a tiny seed-filled lime-like citrus). *Kinilaw na isda* is usually served with whatever fresh white fish happens to be handy, usually *lapu-lapu*

You'll find all kinds of weird and wonderful exotic fruits and vegetables. Centre, a mango vendor.

(garoupa), but it is also made with *tanguigue* (mackeral) and *sunlutan* (beche de mer). Smoked raw *tanguigue* is also served with a dill sauce, in place of Scottish smoked salmon, in many of the top continental restaurants in Manila.

Charcoal or plain grilled fish, whole, in steaks or filleted, is found everywhere in the country, but the varieties of fish available usually astound visitors from big cities in Europe or America. *Bangus* (milkfish) is a rare taste treat anywhere but The Philippines. Also available are *Lapu-lapu, tanguigue, hito* (catfish), *talakitok* (deep sea fish), *kandula* (fresh water fish).

Sinigang is usually billed as the Filipino *boullabaisse* which, though an easily identifying label, gives rather short thrift to this unique Filipino taste. *Sinigang* is a sourish type of soup, with its distinct piquant taste coming from the *kalamansi* or the *sampaloc* (tamarind). Do not confuse it with a hot, spicey taste

which it clearly is not. The ingredients can be *lapu-lapu, tanguigue, kanduli* or *bangus*, along with such delicacies as *sugpo* (prawns) or *hipon* (shrimp), and occasionally *halaan* (clams). *Sinigang* can also be served with beef or pork.

Lobster (actually crayfish) and other seafoods are usually served grilled or cold (in a salad), *calamare* (squid), *pusit* (baby squid), *talaba* (oysters), *lambay* (sea crabs), *alimango* (freshwater crabs) and *tahong* (mussels). The aforementioned *sugpo, hipon* and *halaan* round out the selections from the sea.

Lest you think that seafood is all the Filipinos ever eat, the most popular dish (next to rice) is pork. *Lechon* (suckling pig), usually grilled on a spit over an open fire, (Polynesian style), is an important part of any festival or *fiesta* (of which there are literally more than a thousand a year). After *lechon*, the most popular way of serving pork is not roasted or as pork chops, as in the West, but as pork *adobo*.

The word *adobo* comes from the Spanish word *adobado* (pickled) and refers to any meat or seafood which has been marinated in vinegar laced with spices and garlic, and simmered gently in oil. In the Spanish dish, the whole uncooked loin of pork is cured for weeks in olive oil and spices, but the Filipino version is much quicker, and the "aging" takes place after the meat is cooked.

Any Filipino buffet at the hotels will have pork *adobo* with probably chicken or beef *adobo* as the second choice.

Being in a tropical clime, one would expect the Philippines to be lush with fruit and a glance at any menu or a trip to the market confirms the guess. Some fruits are well-known in the West — *mangoes, honeydew melons watermelons, bananas, pineapples, avocados, papayas* (often called *paw-paw* in other countries) — but one unfamiliar one deserves singling out, the *durian*, the queen of the fruits (the *mango* being the king). *Durian* is to fruit what limburger is to cheese. Found all over Southeast Asia, it is banned in virtually any closed, air-conditioned place, in public (enclosed) places, on planes and ships. It is banned just about anywhere except in the open air market where it is bought.

Durian tastes divine — if you can get it past your nose and into your mouth — but its smell is one of the most pungent odours on this earth. By all means try it, and then have a good wash. Don't try bringing it back to your hotel or ship because if the aroma gets into the air-conditioning system . . . you can imagine the consequences.

One last Filipino delicacy — *balut*. Those with a well-tuned ear will have heard the street vendours shouting *"baaa looot"*. *Balut* are boiled *fertile* duck eggs which are slurped right there at the street stall — the egg (which is more like a duck soup) and the whole little duckling (just two days shy of birth) in a couple of polite gulps. Salt, which is always offered, is a matter of taste. This is definitely not a dish for the squeamish. Politely, *balut* is an acquired taste.

Many of the Filipino style restaurants are *turo-turo* (literally "point-point") which means the Filipino dishes are on display, *a la* self service restaurant, but the restaurants are not necessarily self-service. In the better class ones, after you "turo-turo" your food is brought to your table.

The most famous of the *turo-turo* type restaurants is the **Turo-Turo sa Nayon** in the Nayong Pilipino complex by the Manila International Airport. Another *turo-turo* type is **The Grove**. Actually, you can take your choice whether The Grove is *turo-turo* or table buffet. But the variety of foods there is displayed on tables.

Another type of Filipino restaurant is the *kamayan* variety where you eat with your fingers. The plates are large leaves or palm fronds, sometimes put on a special round woven nipa plate holder. On **Pasay Road** in Makati, there are

Feast your eyes and palate on delectable goodies at the Champagne Room of the Manila Hotel (opposite) and the Playboy Club (above) at the Silahis International Hotel.

three. The **Sinugba** is a Cebuano (from Cebu in the Visayas) seafood restaurant where you eat off off leaves. (There is also a branch in Cebu City.) The **Kamayan** is another restaurant specialising in the finger-to-mouth style, as is the **Bangus**, which serves only milkfish, but in a dozen different ways. The **Josephine** chain of restaurants specialises in seafood, as do the **Zamboanga Restaurants** (in Ermita and Makati). The Zamboanga in Ermita also has a good selection of wines. The small **Buslo** (means "basket") **Restaurant** in Makati is an off-the-beat Filipino seafood restaurant. Two more big restaurants that specialise in Filipino food: The **Sulu Restaurant** and the **Barrio Fiesta**, both in Makati.

Just about every hotel in Manila has some sort of a luncheon buffet which features Filipino food. Some of the hotels also have seafood restaurants which also specialise in some Filipino dishes. The **Badjao** (means "sea gypsy") **Inn** in the **Century Park Sheraton** and the **Pier 7** in the **Philippine Plaza** are both excellent, as is the **Bahia** in the **Inter-continental**. The **Old Manila** in the **Peninsula** and the **Cowrie Grill** in the **Manila Hotel** are seafood specialty restaurants too, but a little more Western. Probably the most expensive of the seafood restaurants is the **Via Mare** in **Makati**.

Manila, being an international and cosmopolitan city, has of course its share of other ethnic eateries, everything in fact from *Canard a l'Orange* to *Peking Duck*.

If *cuisine Française* is your pinnacle of culinary taste, your stay in Manila will be satisfying. **Au Bon Vivant**, with two branches, is well known to Francophiles. It was one of the first, if not *the* first, French restaurant in Manila and is one of only two top French restaurants located outside hotels. The other is **L'Orangerie**, which specialises in **nouvelle cuisine**. The **Table du Baron** (Holiday Inn), **Champagne Room** (Manila Hotel), **L'Hirondelle** (Mandarin) compete with each other for the most elegant French dining.

Continental style restaurants in the hotels also offer gracious dining: Try **The Prince Albert Rotisserie** (Inter-Continental), **Top of the Hilton** (which as the name implies offers a superb view), **Abelardo's** (Philippine Plaza) **Tivoli** (Mandarin) **Capriccio** (Silahis) and the **Quimbaya** (Peninsula).

Spanish food is as popular as you would imagine it to be in a former Spanish colony. The poshest of the posh — and quite probably the poshest eatery in the entire city (which would mean the country), is **The Madrid**. Liveried waiters cater to your every taste and whim in this former antique-filled old mansion-turned-restaurant. Candlelight and strings are featured of course. **Guernica's** in Ermita (also a branch in Makati) is one of the most popular and famous Spanish restaurants, renowned as much for its moderately priced good food as for its Spanish music. **Alba Patio de Makati** is another old favourite with a superb view. **La Bodega** (Peninsula Hotel) and **The Ole** (Manila Garden) round out the choices of Spanish restaurants.

American food? Aside from "fast food emporiums" like **Shakey's Pizza Parlours** (all over the city), various fried chicken (including *Kentucky Fried*), drive-in restaurants, ice cream parlours like the **Coney Island** (in **The Aristrocrat**) and **The Magnolia** and various hotel coffee shops, all that is left is the steak house. Try **Alfredo's**, **Flaming Hot** and **Steak Town**.

The best German food is undoubtedly found in **Hugo's** (Hyatt Regency Hotel), which also has a good selection of game dishes. **The Swiss Inn** has a vast and moderately priced menu full of Swiss, German and Austrian dishes. And especially for those homesick for Deutschland, there is now a **Wienerland** to sample that special chicken.

For Italian food, **La Tasca** is the most elegant and expensive while **La Taverna**, as the name implies, is a less expensive *taverna* type ristorante italiano.

Quite a few Japanese restaurants have sprung up in the past few years. The **Aoi** (Century Park Sheraton), the **Gojinka** (Manila Garden) and the **Kuretake** (Midtown Ramada) are some of the best, as are the **Kaneko** and **New Tokyo** in Makati.

Chinese cooking has influenced Filipino cuisine over the centuries but, strangely, there are few places to get a Chinese meal uninfluenced by the Filipino cuisine. The **Kowloon House** specialises in Cantonese food, including **dim sum**, as does **The Peacock** (Century Park Sheraton), **The Golden Peking** and the **Aberdeen Court** specialise in Northern Chinese cuisine (Peking Duck). The **Mandarin** (Hyatt-Regency and the **Lotus Garden** (Midtown Ramada) are also good Chinese restaurants.

For Mexican food, try **Tia Maria**; Indonesian, the **Borobudor Restaurant**; for Singaporean, the Batik Rama; for Polynesian, the **Luau**; for Turkish, the **Istanbul**; for Vietnamese, the **Saigon**; and for Indian food, the **Kashmir**.

Sample the local cuisine for a taste of the real Philippines. Centre, the kamayan restaurants, where eating with one's hands is de riguer. Right, a local pub in Manila. Following pages, the lobby of the luxurious Manila Hotel.

63

CHINESE RESTAURANTS

Aberdeen Court
7842 Makati Avenue, Makati.
Tel: 98-83-72

Golden Peking
550 E. de los Santos Ave., Quezon City.
Tel: 78-96-31

Kowloon House
PasayRoad, Makati.
Tel: 86-39-06/86-10-03

Lotus Garden
Midtown Ramada.

Mandarin
Hyatt-Regency Hotel.

Peacock
Century Park Sheraton.

FILIPINO AND SEAFOOD RESTAURANTS
(F = Filipino)

Badjao Inn
Century Park Sheraton Hotel.

Bahia
Inter-Continental Hotel.

(F) Bangus
1006 Pasay Rd., Makati.
Tel: 85-27-59

(F) Barrio Fiesta
Buendia St., Makati.
Tel: 87-47-28

(F) Buslo Restaurant
114 Jupiter St., Makati.
Tel: 88-72-04
Cowrie Grill, Manila Hotel.

(F) Grove
5023 P. Burgos St., Makati.
Tel: 89-83-83

(F) Josephine
1800 Roxas Blvd.
Tel: 59-15-50
Also at Greenbelt, Makati.

(F) The Kamayan
47 Pasay Rd. Makati.
Pier, Philippine Plaza Hotel.
Tel: 88-36-04

(F) Sinugba
800 Pasay Rd., Makati.
Tel: 88-02-98

(F) Sulu
Makati Commercial Centre, Makati.

(F) Turo-Turo sa Nayon
Nayong Philipino, The Philippines in Miniature complex, Via Mare, Greenbelt Park, Legazpo St., Makati.
Tel: 85-23-06

FRENCH AND CONTINENTAL RESTAURANTS

Abelardo's
Philippine Plaza Hotel.

Au Bon Vivant
1133 L.Guerrero St., Ermita, Tel: 50-34-05 Also at Makati **Commercial Centre**.
Tel: 87-59-50

Capriccio
Silahis Hotel.

Champagne Room
Manila Hotel.

L'Hirondelle
Mandarin Hotel.

L'Orangerie
89 Zodiac St., Bel-Air IV, Makati.
Tel: 87-89-39

Prince Albert Rotiserie
Inter-Continental Hotel.

Quimbaya
Peninsula Hotel.

Table du Baron
Holiday Inn.

Tivoli
Mandarin Hotel.

Top of the Hilton.
Hilton Hotel.

Hugo's
Hyatt Regency Hotel.

New Swiss Inn
1394 General Luna St., Paco.
Tel: 59-70-81
Also at Coronado Lanes, Makati Commercial Centre.
Tel: 88-79-66

Wienerwald
Greenbelt Park, Makati.

La Tasca
Greenbelt Park, Legazpi St., Makati.
Tel: 86-85-56

La Taverna
1602 M. Adriatico St., Ermita.
Tel: 58-53-72

INDIAN

Kashmir
7844 Makati Ave., Makati.

INDONESIAN

Borobudor
Ground Floor, Luneta Theatre, 1025 L.
Guerrero St., Ermita.
Tel: 58-59-64

JAPANESE

Aoi
Century-Park Sheraton Hotel.

Gojinka
Manila Garden Hotel.

Kaneko
Makati Avenue, Makati.

Kuretake
Midtown Ramada.

New Tokyo
69 Makati Avenue, Makati.
Tel: 87-11-53

MEXICAN

Tia Maria
1038 A.Mabini St., Ermita.
Tel: 59-15-79
with branch on General Luna Street,
Makati.

POLYNESIAN

Luau
7829 Makati Ave., Makati.
Tel: 87-95-43

SINGAPOREAN

Batik Rama
Tradewinds Hotel, South Superhighway,
Makati.
Tel: 85-70-11

SPANISH

Alba Patio de Makati
11th floor, Dona Narcisa Bldg., Makati.
Tel: 86-23-41

La Bodega
Peninsula Hotel.

Guernica's
1326 M.H. del Pilar St., Ermita.
Tel: 50-09-36
branch at 1034 Pasay Road, Makati.
Tel: 88-11-67

Madrid
24-25 E. de los Santos Ave.,
Mandaluyoun, Rizal.
Tel: 79-75-61

Ole,
Manila Garden Hotel

STEAKHOUSES (AMERICAN)

Alfredo's
corner Morato and Lazcano Streets,
Quezon City.
Tel: 97-60-26

Flaming Hot
816 Pasay Rd., Makati.
Tel: 87-74-36

Steak Town
7840 Makati Ave, Makati.
Tel: 88-62-67

TURKISH

Istanbul
corner Makati Ave., and Gen. Luna St.,
Makati

VIETNAMESE

Saigon, corner Makati Ave., and
Constellation St., Makati

Sports

COCKFIGHTING (Sabong)

Mention "Filipino sports," and refer to the "sport of kings," and you'll be pointed to a cockpit, not a race course. Cockfighting (*sabong*) is a way of life in The Philippines. There are cockpits (*sabungan*) in virtually every corner of the archipelago and every Sunday or public holiday the galleries around the central pits are jam-packed with raucous and excited crowds, seated in tiers reaching to the roof.

The pre-fight shouting is directed at the bookmakers (*kristos*), who are minor attractions themselves because of their uncanny ability to absorb all the bets and odds without ever writing anything down. The *kristos* circle the cockpit responding to the shouts (bets) with fingers raised high in a juggling mime of the odds and bets. Thousands of pesos change hands each fight — and there are many fights per day.

Cockfighting is not for the squeamish. Some regard it as so bloody and cruel that it has been banned in many countries.

In the Manila area, the **Pasay City, La Loma** (the city's oldest), and **Marikina** and **Balalaran** (Paranaque), cockpits are probably the best. There are rarely organised tours to the cockpits, but your hotel can easily point you in the right direction in a taxi.

JAI-ALAI

Jai-alai vies with cockfighting as the most popular national sport. Brought to The Philippines 100 years ago from the Basque region in Spain, the sport is said to have actually been invented by the Mayan Indians in South America and imported into Spain hundreds of years ago by Spaniards returning from the colonies. Even in far-away Manila, many of the *pelotaris* (players) are *Basques*. *Jai-alai* is a version of Spanish handball (*pelota*) played between pairs of players, each armed with a *cesta* (wicker basket), laced tightly to the right hand (it seems there are no southpaws in *jai-alai*) so that the *cesta* becomes an extension of the hand. The hard-rubber, hand-made ball is flung against the granite wall at the far end of the court, and like handball or racquetball or squash, is played off the walls on a single bounce. But *jai-alai* differs from other court games in that the ball may reach speeds of 200 kph.

The games begin every afternoon (except Sunday) at 5pm. There are 14 games each session, with a 20 minute break between each for betting.

There is no admission fee to the *fronton* (*jai-alai*) courts so they are jammed every night with everyone from serious afficionadoes to kibbutzers to tourists on a four-hour *fronton* and dinner tour. As there is off-course *jai-alai* betting in Manila, it has been estimated that more than a half-a-million bets are placed daily involving 20 per cent of Manila's population!

PELOTA
Pelota, the game from which *jai-alai* was probably derived, is widely played throughout the country. Most hotels, if they do not have tennis courts, will most certainly have *pelota* courts.

ARNIS DE MANO
Most visitors have heard or seen demonstrations of *kung-fu, karate* or *taekwando*, to name but three of the Asian forms of martial arts, but few people anywhere have ever heard of, and fewer have seen, *arnis de mano* (Filipino stick fighting). The sport is so old that it was first banned by the conquering Spanish. The origin of the sport was the defence of the traveller from robbers armed with a *bolo* (machete). The *tungkod* (stick) is a one metre-long hardwood stick about an inch thick; the opponents are armed with two *tungkods* and *sala* and swing at and parry with each other. Tournaments or exhibitions of *arnis de mano* are infrequent, but do appear. Check the daily newspapers or call the National Arnis Associations (Tel: 23-10-69)

SIPA
Sipa (the word means kick) is a game rarely seen by visitors. It is a variation of volleyball using knees, legs and feet to kick a hollow wicker ball. It is played in singles, doubles or teams of four on a rectangular court divided by a net. Keep an eye out for it if you are travelling in the provinces or near schoolyards.

PALO SEBO
Palo sebo is a *fiesta* sport where contestants climb greased bamboo poles to get a prize perched on the top.

GOLF
For most visitors to The Philippines, golf is the big attraction because the country has some of the finest courses in the world — and several championship courses. Also, because of the climate, golf is an ideal all-year-round sport for the Filipinos.

Within reach of your hotel in Manila are many superb links like the **Wack Wack Golf and Country Club**, the **Manila Golf and Country Club** (The country's oldest), the **Capitol Hills Golf Club**, the **Valley Golf Club**, the **Filipinas Golf and Country Club**, **Nichols Golf Club**, **Fort Bonifacio Golf Club**, **Calatagan Golf Club**, **Batulao Golf Course** and the **Muni** (for Municipal) **Golf Links**. Just about all the clubs have arrangements for visitors (usually only

Sports in the Philippines includes horse fighting at a rodeo at the Davao City Festival (opposite), *and a show of calisthenics at the Cultural Center Complex.*

during weekdays) who are not members of the club or of golf clubs with reciprocal rights, to play for green fees varying from US$6-$25, plus rentals.

SCUBA DIVING
Some of the finest and most exotic underwater areas in the world are in The Philippines. But to make an area a success as a dive spot, organisation on land is needed. The Philippines offers this to such an extent that a visitor with a spare day in Manila can make a quick trip to the resorts in Batangas for a dive, returning to the capital for the evening entertainment. Of course, one of the best and most exciting ways to see and dive the islands is by ship — expedition diving — and there are four diving companies in Manila (See Sports Addresses) which offer a range of diving craft and tours.

The two main centres for diving in the Philippines are Manila and **Cebu**. Manila is the main booking centre, and from the capital you either head for the resorts in Batangas or one of the island resorts (in both cases scuba diving is just one of the recreational facilities offered) or make arrangements for a diving cruise, and normally head for the **Apo Reef** area.

Most people fly to Cebu, though you can sail on an inter-island cruiseliner or freighter. There, you have a choice of basing yourself in **Cebu City** or in one of the resorts on nearby **Mactan Island** (the airport is in fact on Mactan and you cross the toll bridge to Cebu City) or in the tiny village **Moalboal**, on the other side of the island about a three to four hour ride from Cebu City.

The latest virgin territory to open up to organised scuba diving is **Palawan Island** and environs. Sometimes the dive cruises get this far south, but it is easier, quicker and cheaper to fly. The centre for this new diving centre is the new **Hyatt-Rafols Hotel**.

FLYING SCUBA DIVERS CLUB
A note about flying through and to The Philippines with heavy diving gear. Philippine Airlines has the Flying Scuba

Divers Club which will allow a diver to take an extra 30 kilograms above his normal free baggage allowance. To obtain this, either write ahead or go in person when you are in Manila for an application. One small photo and your certification card is all that is needed.

HORSERACING
The original "sport of kings" is also prominent in Manila. Races are held every Wednesday from 5-10pm and all day Saturday, Sunday and Public Holidays at the **Manila Jockey Club** and the Philippine Racing Club. Betting starts as low as two pesos.

SPORTS ADDRESSES
JAI-ALAI

Jai-alai Fronton
Taft Avenue Manila.

Arnis de Mano

National Arnis Association
Rizal Memorial Sports Complex, Vito Cruz, Manila.
Tel: 23-10-69

HORSE-RACING

Manila Jockey Club

San Lazaro Hippodrome
Santa Cruz, Manila.
Tel: 21-16-21

Philippine Racing Club.

Santa Ana Hippodrome
Makati.
Tel: 87-99-51

GOLF

Manila and Environs:

Batulao Golf Course
Pasugbu, Batangas.
Tel: Batulao 40-12-53

Calatagan Golf Course
Calatagan, Batangas.
Tel: 89-40-11
(Punta Baluarte Office)

Capitol Hills Golf Club
Old Balara, Quezon City.
Tel: 97-66-91

Filipinas Golf and Country Club
San Pedro, Laguna.
Tel: 88-85-86 (Manila)
Tel: 842-21-41 (Laguna)

Fort Bonifacio Golf Club
Fort Bonifacio, Rizal.
Tel: 86-28-02

Manila Golf and Country Club
Forbes Park, Makati.

Muni (Municipal) Golf Links
Intramuros, Manila.

Nichols Golf Club
Nichols Air Base, Rizal.
Tel: 83-05-86

Valley Golf Club
Antipolo. Tel: 61-93-54

Wack Wack Golf and Country Club
Mandaluyong.
Tel: 78-40-21

Baguio City:
Baguio Country Club
Baguio City.

Camp John Hay Golf Club
John Hay Airbase.

Bacolod City:
Bacolod Golf and Country Club
Binitin Murcia.

Cebu City:
Cebu Country Club
Banilad. Tel: 92-569

Club Filipino de Cebu
Camputhaw, Lahug.
Tel: 72-727

Davao City:
Apo Golf and Country Club
Bago. Tel: 85-371

Davao City Golf Club
Matina.

Dumaguete City:
Dumaguete Golf and Country Club
Dumaguete.

Iloilo City:
Ilioilo Golf & Country Club
Santa Barbara.

Legazpi, City:
Mayon Imperial Golf Club

Zamboanga City:
Zamboanga Golf and Country Club
Calarian.

BOWLING
Astrobowl
Magallenes Commercial Centre Makatai.

Bowlodrome
Buendia Ave., Makato.

Bowling Inn
Taft Ave., Manila.

Coronado Lanes
Makati Commercial Centre, Makati.

Green Lanes
Greenhills Shopping Centre, Mandaluyong.

Mabini Lanes
A. Mabini Street, Malate.

SCUBA DIVING

Manila.

Dive Boats:

Aquaventure Philippines, P.O. Box 758,
Makati Commercial Centre 3177,
Makati. Tel: 79-86-48 Telex 7227654
SARPH. Cable Aquaventure

Gloria Maris Adventures, Suite 207,
Midtown Ramada Hotel, Ermita. Tel: 59-
62-26 Telex 63920 BETPMMRPW. Attn
Gloria Maris. Cable GLORIS

---

*Many young boys in villages all over the
country dream of becoming a champion
boxer.*

71

Marine Adventure, Mezzanine Floor, Century-Park Sheraton, P.O.Box 117, Manila. Tel: 50-60-41. Ext. 1636, 1638. Telex 27791 CPH PH.

Seaquest Ventures, Philippine Village Hotel, Pasay City. Tel: 80-70-11 Telex 5351 PVHGMCR

DIVE SHOPS

Aqua Tropical Sports: 560 Arkansas Street, Ermita. Tel: 58-95-70. Aquaventure, 908 Pasay Road, P.O. Box 758, Makati Commercial Centre, Makati. Tel: 70-05-88. Telex 7227654 SAR PH.

Bunn's, 928 Passay Road, Makati. Tel: 85-36-76. Telex 3769 MARFEN PN **Dive Asia**, Sampaquita Compound, Grandad Street, Makati. Tel: 89-87-56. St. Moritz, 481-A Flores Street, Ermita. Tel: 59-61-26.

FLYING SCUBA DIVERS CLUB
Tours and Promotions Dept., Philippine Airlines, PAL Administrative Bldg., Legazpi Street, Makati. Tel: 89-59-85, 818-01-01 ext. 245.

Cebu City:

Cebu Divers International, 111 Sepulveda Street, Tel: 93-078 **Club Pacific**, Justice Cabahug Bldg., Tel: 7-9147. Telex PHILCOM 24836 CLP PH.

Moalboal Reef Club Inn, c/- Montebello Villa Hotel, Banilad. Tel: 77-681 Telex 6232 MONTE PU. Cable MONTEBELLO

Neputune Diving and Sea Sports, Gorodro Ave. Tel: 9-06-12 Telex 48007 DIVEIN PM.
Ocean Safari, No. 3 Veloso Apts., Gorordo Avenue, Tel: 70-715. Telex 24729 M/H PH or 8050 SCTARIAT PM.

Reefers Madness, Sceptre Bldg., Gorodro Avenue. PO Box 175. Tel: 91-974, 73-843.

Splash Dive Shop, 14-A J. Osmena Street. Tel: 97-006.

Davao City:

Aquamasters, 75E. Quirino Avenue. Tel: 78-188

Dumaguete City:

Aqua Tours Seahunt. c/- Dr. Angel Alcala, Silliman University Marine Lab. Tel: 59-50-34.

Puerto Princesa, Palawan Island:

Hyatt-Rafols Hotels, c/- Hyatt-Regency Hotel, P.O. Box 2462 Manila. Tel: 80-26-11. Telex PN 3344 (or any Hyatt Hotel Reservation Service). Cable Hyatt, Manila.

Zamboanga City:

Aqua Tropical Sports, Navarro Street, Sam Jose. Tel: 33-73 Julio Luz, c/- Philippine Airlines. Tel: 20-21.

Manila Environs

The most popular half-day or day excursion out of Manila is to **Corregidor Island**, one of the four islands guarding the mouth of Manila Bay, a trip of only 45 km, one way. Corregidor is famous for the 27-day, last-ditch battle between Filipino-American forces and the invading Japanese. After the fall of Bataan on April 9, 1942, Japanese attention turned to the 9.7 square km tadpole-shaped hunk of rock on which 12,000 allied troops held back the Imperial Army in a futile attempt to stop the Japanese tide.

The most nostalgic part of the island tour is the Malinta Tunnel, built between 1922 and 1932, as part of the American effort to fortify Manila Bay. The tunnel proved its worth as it withstood siege by land, sea and air bombardment, which at that time was the most intensive bombardment of a single target ever known by man. Soon after the Japanese invaded on December 21, 1941, Manila was declared an open city and the American commissioner and the military, led by General Douglas MacArthur, moved their headquarters to Corregidor. About 76,000 Filipino and American troops were deployed in a holding action against the Japanese armies in Bataan and Corregidor.

The organised Corregidor half-day tours costs about US$30 for four hours, which includes an hour's hydrofoil ride each way and two hours on the rock. It is easy enough to go by yourself. The Hover Ferry Terminal is behind the **Cultural Centre of the Philippines** on Roxas Boulevard. It costs 135 pesos (children under seven, half), which includes a tour of the island. Departures 8 am and 1:30 pm daily, but the ticket office is open 7am-6pm daily.

Some of the tour agencies run a Corregidor/Beach tour combination, half day and whole day. The intrepid can camp out overnight on Corregidor and then take the ferry to **Mariveles**, four kilometres north in **Bataan** (or skip the camping entirely), to see the rest of the "fall of the Philippines story," returning to Manila by bus along the famous 88 km Bataan Death March route between **Mariveles** and **San Fernando** (POW Camp O'Donnell), on which 10,000 Filipino and American POW's died.

An excursion of a much happier sort is one to **Pagsanjan** (pronounced *pag-san-han*), in **Laguna Province** on the southeast side of **Laguna de Bay**, only a

The brighter side of tourism in the Philippines. Opposite, the lobby of the Manila Hotel. Above, the facade of the Metropolitan Theatre.

two to three hour drive from Manila. The small town of Pagsanjan is located by the river of the same name and the whole idea of the expedition is to hop aboard some *bancas* (native canoes) paddled by expert *banceros* (boatmen), and battle upstream for about 40 to 50 minutes through 14 sets of rapids until you come to the 91-metre **Pagsanjan Falls**, which are in fact the Magdapio Falls, if the truth be known. Here you can rent space on a raft, capable of holding eight to 10 people and, using a fixed wire, come very close to the falls and actually slip in behind. You can also get off the raft and swim behind the falls and since the spray drenches you anyway, you may as well have a swim! You are in a gorge here (Pagsanjan Gorge National Park) so the only way out is by river, shooting the 14 rapids in a hair-raising, hell-for-leather run controlled (by the *banceros*) back down to the calm water by the river landing at the Pagsanjan Rapids Hotel. The average tour (about 9 hours), with (Manila) hotel pickups is around us$30, but you can take a public bus there and rent your own *banca* and *banceros* for considerably less. The Pagsanjan annual fiesta is December 12.

Many people also take an overnight visit to Hidden Valley, also in Laguna. The resort is four kilometres north of the town of **Alaminos**, about a two-hour drive from Manila. A private plantation belonging to the Don Eufrocino Roxas family since 1918, this pleasant verdant corner has natural warm, cold and "just right" soda springs from nearby **Mt. Makiling**, a 1090-metre extinct volcano with a 41-metre deep crater. The springs have been dammed into natural swimming holes and connected with each other by concrete paths, so everything is accessible with the minimum of effort. There are cottages available for overnight stays.

The entrance fee is 30 pesos (with lunch) per person. No picnics permitted. Bookings through any travel agent (the 10-hour tour is about us$30) or directly through the Manila Office.

There are other great natural attractions in the area. Just before the town of **Los Banos** is **Alligator** or **Enchanted Lake**, a crater lake (again from volcanic Mt. Makiling) about 60 km from Manila. (There are no more alligators left, but the name somehow sticks).

Caliraya Lake is an artificial lake (actually a reservoir) in Laguna, about 112 km from Manila and yet another lovely spot to while away a couple of days. The **Lagos de La Sierra Resort** has luxurious digs while the **Nayong Kalikayan Caliraya** (means "Village of Nature") is more rustic with its cabins built on stilts over the lake waters. The **South Superhighway** provides speedy transportation from Manila to this whole Laguna area.

Another of the half-day tours is the four-hour **Tagaytay Ridge** trip about 60 km from Manila in **Batangas Province**. Tagaytay is a ridge, 686 metres above sea level, overlooking a magnificent vista of the blue waters of **Lake Taal**, the active **Taal Volcano** on Volcano Island

and the apple-green waters of the "lake within a lake", **Yellow Lake** (actually it is in the crater), about 15 km distant.

The town of Taal was founded in 1572 by Augustinian friars and was originally on the south edge of the lake. It was called Lake Bombon then, supposedly from the sounds of the volcano's belching and burping. The town was destroyed in the 18th century and reincarnated in its present location. The **Taal Church** (1856) is on a hill overlooking the **Plaza**, reached by a wide flight of steps, and is worth a visit.

The Tagaytay Ridge is as close as you are going to come to the lake and volcano if you go by the standard organised half day tour (about US$16-$18). The full day tour (US$30) continues down to the town of **Agoncillo** on the lake's edge from where you can take a 30-minute *Banca* ride to Volcano Island, where the Taal Volcano is located.

From Tagaytay, you can head down to the coast to the popular beach resorts in **Nasugbu** on the west coast of Batangas Province. You can easily do Tagaytay and head for the resorts in one day, but it is a bit much to cope with if you include Taal and Volcano Island.

In Nasugbu Bay, there's the **Maya-Maya Reef Club** (some of the tour companies run day-tours, either scuba diving or just swimming, to this resort, about 10 hours, for US$40), the **White Sands Beach Resort** and the **Batulao Village Club**, all approximately 104 km or two to three hours by car from Manila.

In **Anilao** (Batangas) are clustered the scuba diving resorts of **Dive 7000**, **Divemasters-Seafari**, and **Aqua-Tropical Sports**. These three run beach, *banca* and cruise dives.

Also in Batangas is the **Punte Baluarte** resort and the adjacent **Calatagan Golf Club** (shared facilities) on the tip of the Calatagan peninsula, 125 km or about a two to three hour ride (via Tagaytay Ridge) from Manila.

Some of the other big resorts in this area are reached by private plane from the domestic airport. Balesin Island is 96 km due east of Manila in Lamon Bay (about 30 minutes away by plane) while **Sicogan Island Club**, in the western Visayas, is 403 km or two and a half hours away by plane. (Sicogon can also be reached by private plane from **Bacolod City**).

Even the **Club Pacific** on **Cebu Island** and the **Tambuli Beach Resort** on **Adjacent Mactan Island**, both an hour's flight on a PAL jet to Cebu City, are marketed out of Manila, and you can probably reach them in about the same time it takes you to drive the three hours south from the capital. And for those who want resort facilities while staying in Manila, try the **El Grade/Tropical Palace Resort Hotel**, within commuting distance of the city.

The Yigan Cathedral stands serene in front of a quiet reflecting pool in Ilocos Sur.

Baguio

Baguio, the cool summer capital of The Philippines and provincial capital of Benguet Province, nestles in the Central Cordilla Mountain range at a height of 1524 metres, about a four to five hour ride via the zigzagging Kennon Road or an hour's flight north of Manila. Sculpted terraces, like the hill stations of India, abound the area and the temperature is about 10-15°C cooler than in Manila and on the plains. The scent of thousands of pine trees fills the air.

The tradition of escaping to Baguio to avoid the summer heat in Manila is only about 70 years old and was started by the Americans. Before that, Baguio was only a tiny hamlet called Kafagway and the neighbouring (and larger) village of **La**

Trinidad, now the province's "vegetable garden," was the provincial capital.

Mansion House is the summer residence of the president of The Philippines and its front gate is said to be an exact copy of the gates guarding Buckingham Palace in London. **The Chinese Bell Temple** is a blend of Buddhist, Taoist, Confucian and Christian architecture and has to be seen to be believed. The view from **Mines View Park** out over the valley and mountains is superb.

But shopping is one of the main attractions, aside from the weather, of Baguio. The main street, **Session Road**, is lined with shops, and ends in the big long-house style City Market, where you can buy everything from fresh strawberries

and strawberry jam, to baskets from the hilltribes and hand-woven items. (Maybe the first purchase should be a hand-woven *bayong* or tote bag, to carry everything). There is also a small army surplus section if you want to replenish anything. Just near the City Market, between **Kayang** and **Albano Streets** is a two-storey shopping complex where basketware, silver filigree and Igorot hilltribe woven items are also found. The open market at Mines View Park is another good place to shop.

Baguio is the "silver filigree" capital of The Philippines, but the price is determined by the weight of the item, not by its intricacy or design. If you are buying a lot of silver filigree souvenirs or jewellery, it would pay to compare prices with the more expensive shops in the hotels. The **St. Louis Silver Shop** is a good place to start, then try **Philippine Treasures, Tesitas** and **Pilak**. The **Easter School Weaving Room** has some of the best stocks of Igorot weavings. And for a good selection of antiques and the various types of baskets (all sizes) from the various mountain tribes, try the **Little Green House, Madam Chen's** and **Carma Antiques**. Also have a look at the Benquet display centre in **La Trinidad**. Bargain like mad, especially in the markets.

Baguio has three excellent and famous golf courses, two of which are open to the public, the **Baguio Country Club** and the **Camp John Hay Course**. The third one is the private **Presidential Course**.

The casino at the **Resort Pines Hotel** packs visitors in nightly. The posh **Hyatt-Terraces Hotel**, with its nine-storey terraced atrium, has one of the best drinking bars in town, the **Hunter's Pub**; another good watering hole is the **Keg Room** in the **Nevada Hotel**. Japanese food is best in the **Hanazono** at the Hyatt-Terraces. The **Swiss Grill** (Pines Resort) and the **Plaza Rotisserie** are the two best European restaurants followed by **Casa Mario** for Spanish cuisine. The **Baguio Mandarin, Star Cafe** and **Mountain Peak** all offer reasonable Chinese fare.

The two big discos are the **Crystal Cave** (Hyatt-Terraces) and the **Sadiwan** (Resort Pines). Folk music is played nightly at the **Fire Place, Country Tavern** and the **Gingerbread Man**. And lastly, the strip of girlie bars along **MacArthur Highway** is as close as you will ever get to the bars of Ermita.

Slightly farther afield from Baguio proper are the **Crystal Caves** (supposedly ancient Igorot burial caves), the **Asin Hot Springs** and the Lourdes Grotto, perched up atop 225 steps.

Who needs a bank when one can wear one's savings on one's arm? Here, a woman from the Tauaandig *tribe of Bukidnon.*

The Resort Pines Hotel has its own daily air-conditioned bus service between Baguio and Manila (c/o Mantours, Inter-Continental Hotel, Makati, Tel: 818-38-49) as does Sarkies Tours (Midland Plaza, M. Adriatico St., Ermita, Tel: 59-76-58). You can also get to Baguio by train to the town of **Alaminos** then the bus up the zigzag mountain roads.

Baguio is also the gateway to the Northern section of Luzon. The **Dangwa Bus Company** has daily runs up to **Bontoc** and **Banaue**, as does **Patranco North Express**. The **Philippine National Railways Bus Company**, the **Philippine Rabbit Lines**, **Marcitas Liner**, **Victory Bus**, **Overland Bus** and **Dagupan Bus Companies** all run scheduled services either back to Manila or down to the coast towards **La Union Province**. For an up-to-date bus schedule with phone numbers and addresses, check with the **Tourism Office** on **Governor Pack Road**.

Cebu

Cebu City is the second largest in The Philippines and the oldest, because it is here that Ferdinand Magellan landed in 1521, and here where he met his untimely demise. It is a city of about half a million people, about a quarter of the entire population of the province, and lies 588 km south of Manila.

The city sports the oldest fort in the country, **San Pedro**, construction of which was started by Miguel Lopez de Legazpi in 1565 and finally completed in 1738. It now houses the Department of Tourism and a small museum. It is also the home of the oldest university, **San Carlos**, founded in 1565 and the oldest monument, **Magellan's Cross**, said to have been actually placed there by the famed navigator/captain himself in 1521. (It was on that spot that the first Mass was said). The two oldest streets in the country, **Colon** and **Magallanes**, are also in Cebu City. It also has the oldest (459 years) Sto. Nino, which was Magellan's gift to the **Muslim** Queen Juana on her conversion and baptism.

Any tour of the city will end up as a religious trip into its Spanish past.

Other sites in the city include the **San Agustin Church** (1565 and restored 1975), the chapel of the Last Supper in the **Mandaue Parish Church** (13 life-size statues dating from the Spanish period) and two Chinese temples, the **Taoist Temple** and the **Phu Sian Temple**, both in **Beverly Hills**.

Part of Cebu City's claims to fame for tourism are the beach resorts of **Tambuli** and **Hadsan** on nearby **Mactan Island**, the **Sta. Rosa Resort** on **Olongo Island**, and the **Club Pacific, Marlou Island** and **Balili Beach Resorts** on Cebu.

The best buys in Cebu are guitars, ukeleles or mandolins, all hand-made on Mactan Island in the *barrios* of **Maribago** and **Abuno**. The two biggest stores are **Susing** and **Lilang**, but it is possible to find a working artisan sitting under his house on stilts in some tiny *barrio* and bargain for a guitar right on the spot.

In addition to jeepneys and taxis, there

Gamblers invariably head for the floating casino moored at Pier 1 or the **Jai-alai fronton** (stadium).

The **Inner Circle**, the **Altitude, Love City**, and Disco Pad (Magellan Hotel) are the best discos while **Bachelor's Too** is the best girlie bar. The **Sigay Bar** (Magellan) has excellent live music. And for folk music, try the **Marlboro** and **Andy's Folk Houses**. Being a sophisticated big city, there is also an abundance of massage/sauna parlours.

Davao

Though the **Davao** area has a long Muslim history, it was only in 1847 that the Spanish managed to land a force sufficient to colonise it, three years after the Sultan of Mindanao ceded the area. Obviously the Muslims resident at the mouth of the Davao River when the Spanish first arrived, led by a Spanish solider-of-fortune named Don Uyanguren, were not informed because they continued to fight for their land from the moment the Spanish waded ashore.

The Spanish influence lasted only to the turn of the century when, in 1900, an American administration took over. But that 53 years of Spanish influence was enough to establish Davao as a powerful Christian enclave in Muslim Mindanao.

are motorised trishaws (50¢ for three kilometres) and PU's, tiny four-seater cars with no meters which travel within the city for a two-peso fare. The two-wheel traditional horse-drawn carts are called *tartanilla* and there are still a few of these around.

Cebu City has two excellent golf courses, the **Cebu Country Club** and the **Club Filipino de Cebu**, and it even has a winery called **St. Mary's Grape Wine Factory**, which should give you an idea of the taste. St. Mary's produces three wines, a sweet, a medium red and a dry white.

The city sports some excellent eateries. **Sinugba** (with a branch in Manila) is the most traditional, serving Cebuano style seafood *Kamayan* in the fingers-to-mouth style. **The Fishing Village** is another excellent seafood eatery in this style. For continental food, **Eddie's Log Cabin**, the **Beehive, Puerto Gallera** (Magellan Hotel) and the La Escondida (Montebello Villa Hotel) are the best.

If it weren't for Magellan, who knows what religion in the Philippines would be like today? Centre, *a mural in Cebu City depicts Magellan planting the first cross in the Philippines.* Above, *the Baguio Cathedral, Baguio.*

Davao has two main claims to fame. It bills itself as the world's largest city, covering some (24,000 hectares). It is also known throughout the country as the "durian city."

The first impression of Davao, a bustling harbour city of some 750,000, is that of a rich boom town, and that is fairly correct since most of the primary industries (logging, mining etc) prevalent in Mindanao have their headquarters in Davao.

Though Davao is the third largest city in the country, it is considered a bit far off the tourist beat, even though it is only a 90-minute flight from Manila. Getting around Mindanao these days is a bit difficult because of the on-going war between the central government and the Moro National Liberation Front, though this side of Mindanao is more open to travellers than the other side. This may be your only chance to see a Muslim village and there are several to choose from.

San Jose Village on **Samal Island** (reached after an hour's ride in a pumpboat hired from **Sta. Ana Pier** for 50 pesos or by organised tours for 100 pesos) would provide a pleasant outing, including a picnic and swim if desired. You will see signs all over Davao for the **Aguinaldo Pearl Farm**, also on Samal Island, and the boatmen invariably head there. Skip it. It is not worth the time or trouble. There is another small Muslim village on stilts (actually a collection of villages in the city) on **Quezon Boulevard** near **Magsaysay Park**. You can wander through there and even take a pumpboat out to the farthest reaches or the

mosques.

Davao does have several good beaches — **Times, Godo, Salakot/Talomo, Victorio's Guino-o** beaches, between four and 23 km from the city and accessible by regular jeepney costing two pesos, or by taxi for about 15 pesos. **Talomo Beach** was the scene of the Japanese landings in 1942, followed by the American landings three years later. Times Beach is the worst of these black sand beaches, but they steadily improve as you go farther out. Also, there are small Muslim fishing communities scattered along the way which are quite interesting.

On that same beach road is Davao's religious shrine, the **Shrine of the Holy Infant Jesus of Prague**. The story is that the wife of Davao's mayor had a vision and evenutally went to Prague with her son to bring this icon back.

Another Muslim village is at **Wangan, Calinan**, about 32 km from town. These people belong to the Bagobo tribe and are said to be among the original inhabitants of the area. They do put on a special show, complete with their native dress, but this is by pre-arrangement. If you pop in unannounced, you will see "native" T-shirts and jeans!

Two other of the city's sights: The **Lon Wa Temple**, the biggest Buddhist temple in Mindanao as befits the largest Chinese population centre on the Island, and the **Caroland Resort**, which was actually developed from the Inigo Fish Farms, if you want to see some of the world's largest and laziest carp.

The shopping is excellent in Davao. And it is virtually one-stop shopping. Head for the **Aldevinco Shopping Centre** which has a superb selection of tiny shops selling tribal handicrafts, weavings and brassware. The **Razul, d'Diamond, House of Antiques** and **Maranao** shops offer everything from silver inlaid betalnut boxes to a variety of brass boxes, chests, batiks — just about anything. The first store, Razul's, has the biggest selection of brassware, but you really have to dig. The **Mindanao Souvenir Shop** has a few **santos**, which are rare in this part of the Philippines, and **Bagobo** skirts, manaya cloth, plus blouses from the Ata and B'laan tribes.

The biggest selling hand-woven item seems to be the Maranao Tribe's *malong*, a long piece (about 12 metres) of woven and highly decorated cloth joined lengthwise to create a tube or cylinder and worn as a shirt or a dress. The colours are vivid purples, blues, yellows, reds and greens. Bargain like mad for everything. The first price mentioned is well over two or three times what you should pay. And the final price should be half to a third of the Manila price.

The second most popular religion here is Islamism. Here, *the Quiapo Mosque, downtown Manila.*

Perhaps the most exciting "thing to do" in Davao is the trek to the top of the dormant volcano of Mt. Apo, The Philippines' tallest peak at 2,954 metres. Agencies run the four-day trek for 900 pesos per person with a minimum of three in the party. However, it is possible to make the trek to the top for considerably less by going by bus first to **Kidapawan** in **North Cotabato** or **Digos** in **Davao del Sur** yourself. Though the two paths to the top are different, they both pass through hot springs, magnificent lakes, verdant forests, lush with wild orchids and home of the rarely seen *haribon* (monkey-eating eagle). Just before reaching the peak, the forest becomes dwarfed and disintegrates into shrub country. The smell of sulphur fills the air as the fumes escape through the mountain vents.

The top hotel in Davao or, for that matter, in this part of Mindanao, is the **Davao-Insular Hotel**, An Inter-Continental hotel which is virtually a small resort all by itself. The area around the hotel is dotted with neatly spaced coconut trees with knotches all the way up to the top and every morning the *mananguete* climb the tree to collect the sap, *tuba*, which is gathered in a bamboo tube attached to his waist and later made into a potent drink. Have a snort of *tuba* on the spot or be civilised and order one at the bar. The choice is yours.

The best restaurant in the town is **La Parilla**, a barbecue on the lawns of the Davao-Insular served in quasi-*kamayan* (by hand) style. The hotel also has two other "continental" restaurants, **Maranaw** and **Mandaya**. The Apo View Hotel, the other major hotel in the city, features a poolside barbecue and the **Mikado**, a Japanese restaurant. For a real "Filipino" treat, try the native food stalls along **Quezon Boulevard**, near Sta. Ana Harbour. The *kinilaw* (raw marinated tuna), or squid, or barbeque chicken legs are delicious and cheap.

The **Vinta Bar** (Davao-Insular) and the **Penc Bar** (Apo View) are good music bars. The **One Down** (Apo View), the **Subway Disco** (D'Fabulous Venee's Hotel) and **Studio 7** (Maguinanao Hotel) are the three big discos, as well as **Discolandia** in town. The **Casino**, one of the prime attractions for an evening's entertainment, is in the Davao-Insular Hotel. The girlie bars or "supperclub/night clubs" as they are called in Davao, are all along **MacArthur Highway**. Try **Marrakesh**, **Jimm's** and **Jayside**.

Zamboanga

Zamboanga truly is a City of Flowers. Virtually the entire city is a lush garden of flowers and orchids of every conceivable type, so it is naturally famous throughout the country as a beauty spot and the "garden of The Philippines." Even tiny **barrios** outside the main city have carefully kept gardens and the roads are lined with plants and blooms, placed in small containers or discarded tins.

The centre-piece of the Spanish conquest of the area was **Fort Pilar**, designed by a Jesuit engineer, Father Melchor de Vera. The walls are more than a metre thick and it has withstood sieges over the years by Muslim, Dutch, British and Portuguese forces. The Spanish needed some sort of a fort because they fought sporadic Moro wars against Muslim natives until the Americans took over.

With the arrival of the Americans in 1898, Fort Pilar became a barracks, and today it houses soldiers from the Philippine Constabulary based in Zamboanga because of the troubles.

The most famous of the early American governors was General John J. "Black Jack" Pershing, one of the heroes of World War I. The city's Spanish style **Central Plaza** was renamed in his honour in 1915.

Zamboanga was once a jumping-off place to head south to **Basilan**, **Jolo** or the **TawiTawi Islands**, and all points further south in the **Sulu Sea**. Today, the city of Zamboanga is an isolated peninsula

artificially cut off from the rest of the island by military roadblocks. On the west coast you can only go about 20 km, just past the **San Ramon Prison** and **Penal Farm** before you are stopped. On the east coast, the road is blocked after **Taluksangay**, a Muslim village on stilts about 23 km up the road, and to the north, the boundary is the far side of lovely **Pasonanca Park** which adjoins the city. To follow the road beyond on either coast or to fly south, foreigners need permission from the Department of National Defence in Manila, though there are tales of foreigners getting off in **Jolo** and remaining a few days until being politely kicked off the island by the military.

Though three-quarters of the 300,000 people living in Zamboanga are Christians, the Muslim minorities are the most colourful. Most apparent are the *Badjaos*, the sea gypsies or boat people who spend much of their lives at sea, and the *Samals*, the coastal fishermen whose villages are the ones normally shown as the "Muslim village."

The large Muslim village-on-stilts, seen clearly from the ramparts of Fort Pilar with its silver-domed mosque, is actually three separate groupings of Muslims, Campo Muslim, Rio Hondo and Sahaya, housing Tausugs, Samals and some Badjaos.

One of the more pleasant excursions in Zamboanga is the one-hour trip out to **Sta Cruz Island**. The *bancas* hold six people and cost 50 pesos and can be rented along **Cawa Cawa** Boulevard, or **Justice Lim Blvd**, as it was previously known, or at the **Lantaka Hotel**. The island has beautiful clear waters and virtually deserted beaches, except for a small Samal fishing community and a small Badjao cemetery — quite a pleasant outing. (The tour agency price for this outing is about double).

Other tours include trips to the **Taluksangay Muslim Village** (90 pesos

---

When the sea gypsies aren't in a boat, they are on the water in their houses on stilts. Above, *Rio Ondo in Zamboanga City.*

for half-day) and the Labuan fishing village tour, (120 pesos for half-day), which is 35 km from town and the farthest point you can reach. (Tour vehicles are allowed through the roadblock to visit **Labuan**).

Zamboanga does, however, have some excellent shopping and it is probably the one place in the country (Manila and the various Duty Free Shops included) where you can get reasonably priced, untaxed luxury goods — everything form clothes and shoes to Samsonite cases and cassette radio recorders. The reason for this largesse is the sophisticated local barter trade. Swift *kumpits* (long motorboats) whip across to neighbouring **Sabah** with rice and sugar and return with the goodies, completely ignoring the various customs duties. This was once an illegal, but uncontrollable, trade since the economy of the area depends to a large extent on duty-free cheaper goods, but has now been legitimised. The famous **Barter Market** by the waterfront burned down in a spectacular pre-Christmas conflagration in 1979, only to re-appear a few days later under official auspices by the name of **Pasanoca Shopping Mall**, located just below the city by the **Zamboanga Plaza Hotel**. Two more sites have also been designated for the Barter Market, next to the Lantaka Hotel and by the airport. So there are now three Barter Markets.

A good place to visit for Muslim handicrafts (the barter markets offer only new consumer goods) is the **Flea Market**, cunningly located behind the meat section of the **Public Market** through which you have to walk. Brassware, handwoven items including *malongs*, betalnut boxes, are featured. Another shopping area is the **Yakan Weaving Village**, just seven kilometres from the city. The Yakans are from Basilan Island and are farmers, not seafarers or fishermen. They sell various lengths of cloth, clothes and bags in vivid primary colours, all of which are woven on the spot. Unlike most of the people in Zamboanga, they are quite forceful with

their sales pitch and do not hesitate to give you an earbashing if you do not buy or bargain too hard. For shells, try the **Rocan**, **San Luis** or **Laygan** shops.

One of the most spectacular places to visit is **Pasonanca Park**, encompassing 57 hectares. The name is a contraction of three words — *paso de nanca*, which means "Pass of the Jackfruit," and the *nanca* trees are all over the park. The park was founded in 1911 by Governor Pershing and has natural swimming holes, scout camps and its *piece de resistance*, a tree-house.

The Pasonanca Park Tree House is built about 12 metres off the ground in a giant acacia tree, and reached by a spiral metal staircase. The single room is a compact apartment complete with stove, fridge, pantry, table, two bunks, toilet and shower cubicle and a telephone. Started in 1960, the Tree House has literally seen

hundreds of guests. Write or cable the Mayor, c/o City Hall, Zamboanga for reservations. Stays are normally limited to one or two nights. The pantry is usually stocked and the guest is required to replenish what has been used.

You cannot leave Zamboanga until you have a drink in **Talisay Bar**, built around a giant acacia tree in the garden of the **Lantaka-by-the-Sea** (to give it its full name) **Hotel**, formerly the **Bayout Hotel**. (Though the outdoor bar is now fixed up a bit, it was once described as "a place the *African Queen* would have tied up to, if Bogie and Hepburn could have made it that far!")

The seafood, as you can imagine, is superb in this part of the country and the **Zamboanga Plaza Hotel's Kamayan sa Plaza Restaurant** offers an excellent menu of fresh seafood "turo turo" (point-point) style. The **Jamboangan Bar**

(Zamboanga Plaza) is a pleasant bar with music. The disco scene is at the **Cobweb** (Zamboanga Plaza), **Le Concorde (Zambayan Hotel)** and the **Disco-Pub (Imperial Hotel)**. The best of a bad lot of girlie-bar strip joints (bump'n grind behind a sheet in silhouette) are the **Crazy Horse** and the Log House. The casino in the Zamboanga Plaza, like the casinos in the other Philippine cities, is the centre of a normal night's entertainment. There are plenty of massage parlours, and a room service is offered in the hotels with a "20 percent discount for a married couple massage!"

This will appeal to those who dream of throwing it all away and retreating to that tiny island in the Pacific. Here, a sea-gypsy village in Tawi-tawi. Following pages, Brooks Point Beach in Southern Palawan.

Passport to Adventure
Off the Tourist Track

Vigan

The northern Luzon city of Vigan is a time warp into Spanish colonial life a century ago. Like the Latin Quarter of New Orleans, the *mestizo* (means half-Filipino, or Chinese-Filipino) district of Vigan sprouted with magnificent Spanish style houses and mansions, as the *nouveaux riches* Chinese-Filipino traders tried to outdo the "pure" Spanish of the city.

Many of these magnificent dwellings, along with their narrow, cobblestone streets opening onto wide Spanish plazas, are still preserved and it is this architectural throwback to a century ago that gives Vigan its flavour and fame. They all have high-arched doorways with sufficient clearance to take a carriage — and if you are lucky, perhaps someone will admit you to the inner courtyard during your ride in a *calesa*, the horse

drawn rigs which still ply Vigan's streets. Once inside the courtyard, the gentry disembarked and the horses went to the stables and the people into the house, all within the confines of the high walls. While the lower part of the house was made of stone, the upper part was normally of wood with balconies overlooking the streets. It is an eerie feeling to walk through this old section of Vigan as the sun moves across the sky, dividing streets with the long shadows, and you can hear the clip-chopping of a *calesa* echoing off the stone. One expects a "Spanish" Don and a Doña to come out in their carriage right before your eyes.

There are not many hotels in Vigan, but try the **Vigan Hotel** and the **Cordilla Inn**, both housed in large mansions in the old quarter, and each sandwiched in between two equally old and ornate

mansions. If you have the time, visit the **Cathedral of St. Paul** (dating from 1574, rebuilt in 1641, renovated in 1790 and completed in 1800), the **Archbishop's Palace** (founded 1783), the **Ayala Museum** in the home of Father Jose Burgos, a *mestizo* priest martyr — to Philippine independence — executed in 1872 by the Spanish and the **Syquia Mansion**, one of the most elaborate and well preserved houses, built in 1830.

Further north, **Laoag** is a fairly large city and a bustling market town. Its Spanish history dates from the 17th century and there are still *calesas*, and the even more antique *tartanillas* (six-seater horse-drawn carriages), plying the streets. President and Prime Minister, Ferdinand E. Marcos, was born in nearby **Sarrat**, seven kilometres from Laoag. The house in which he was born and lived is now the "Marcos Museum."

Northern Luzon

There are gruelling, zig-zagging, all-day marathon rides over mountain roads once you leave **Baguio** and head into the splendour of **Northern Luzon**, but the experience is worth every bone-jarring minute of them. Baguio City is the dividing line between those on a quick tour and those who wish to explore. The northern mountain areas are perfect for those who want to get off the beaten tourist track and explore, but not *too* far off the track.

The **Halsema Highway** out of Baguio is the path north to most destinations. The major destination is **Banaue** and the fabled rice terraces and you could do it in nine to 10 hours of steady driving, but you would be missing quite a bit if you rushed that much.

For a pleasant and slower trip, head north as far as **Mt. Data**, an eight-room lodge run by the Philippine Tourism Authority, nestling pleasantly at 2,256 metres with a magificent view. (The superlative adjectives used to describe the various mountain views from the various sites begin to lose their meaning from over-use. But do not let that influence you against the beauty of Northern Luzon and the **Grand Cordillera Mountain Range**.) Mt. Data is about halfway, by distance, to Banaue, and two-thirds of the way to **Bontoc**, one of the major towns of the range. To fill out a pleasant day with something bizarre, include **Kabayan** (in Benquet Province) and the "mummy caves" nearby.

For the few hardy trekkers and mountain climbers, the way to Mt. Pulag, the sacred Igorot mountain which is the highest peak in Luzon at 2,932 metres, is via **Kabayan**. Most of your supplies will have to be bought in Baguio, but some can be replenished in Kabayan.

Kabayan is famous for its burial caves, approximately 80 of them scattered throughout the **Mt. Timbac** area and the mummies therein, some supposedly dating back 400-500 years. The mummies are from the Ibaloi tribe. Many are unwrapped, but all were at one time folded into foetal position in wooden coffins made from tree trunks. Some are still so well preserved you can see the tribal tattoos. The preservation process, incidentally, has long been lost to history. Specimens of the mummies can be seen at the **Kabayan Museum** (in the town hall) or at the **Odpas** (Ordas) and **Tinongchol** (**Tenonchol**) burial caves. The former has a chamber where hundreds of skulls are piled up.

Again, if you have the time, it would pay to make a small detour to the village of **Sagada**, which, in addition to magnificent scenery, also has its own burial caves. They are a bit out of town, but easy to find. Dangling from the cliffs on the edge of town are more coffins, separated from the ones in the burial caves, presumably with mummies inside and presumably put there to keep the mummies from predators or thieves. (If

Baubles, bangles, beads (and note the pull tab from a beer can in his right ear), this Ifugao chieftain is dressed in his Sunday best for the Grand Canao Festival in Banaue.

you decide to overnight, accommodation is available at **St. Joseph's Guest House**).

It is another three to four hours to **Banaue**, where the most famous sight in all of Northern Luzon awaits you — the rice terraces, some of which stretch another 305 metres above Banaue, making them almost a mile (1.6 km) high! It is no exaggeration to say the rice terraces are a sight to behold. The Filipinos proudly declare them the Eighth Wonder of the world. Covering an area of some 259 square km. the terraces date back more than 3,000 years and were originally started by a nomadic tribe of Mongolians — according to one theory. Work has not stopped on those terraces in all those years and new ones are continually being made. The mountainside is hacked out and retaining walls built with the rock to enclose small rice paddies. Man-made waterfalls take care of the irrigation. Along with rice, fish are raised.

If you have an opportunity to stay over, do so. The **Banaue Hotel/Hostel** is a small establishment with two types of accommodation (20 individual hotel rooms plus dormitory hostel facilities) run by the Philippine Tourism Authority and is the best Banaue has to offer.

To the South

Bicolandia, the six provinces which make up the southern tip of Luzon Island, is the southern route destination for those who want to get away from Manila.

Naga City, the "Rice Bowl" of Bicolandia, which dates its Spanish "founding" back to 1575, is one of the main stops on the railway line which runs almost to **Legazpi**. Naga City is best known for its Penafrancia Festival, which culminates in a spectacular fluvial procession along the **Naga River** (third weekend in September) when the Virgin of Penafrancia, the Patron Saint of Bicolandia, is returned to her shrine by the river. Thousands of Bicolanos and tourists crowd the banks and bridges to see the seaborne procession pass. It is the most crowded time to visit Naga City, but obviously the most exciting.

But the real reason people venture this far south is the **Mayon Volcano**, a lethal beauty with a perfect cone and a habit of

Opposite, *rice terraces transform a mountain into a gigantic piece of sculpture in Sagada, Igorot Land.* Above, *thatched roofs protect from the sun, while wall-less houses take advantage of cooling breezes in Poitan Village, 7 kilometres away from the Banaue Hotel.*

erupting periodically. The 2423 metre high volcano — the name comes from the Bicol word *magayon* meaning "beautiful" — dominates the landscape of most of Albay Province and all of Legazpi City.

Still smoking and fuming, the volcano has erupted more than 40 times in recorded history. The first eruption was in 1616. The worst recorded eruption took place on February 1, 1814 — one with such force that it buried the entire town of **Cagsawa**, just outside the town of **Daraga**.

The present Daraga town, 5.4 km from Legazpi, was moved because of the 1814 eruption to its present location. During that same eruption, the town of **Camalig** 14.5 km from Legazpi City caught fire in parts. More than 1,200 people perished when Cagsawa was buried and all that is left now is the blackened church steeple (the church dated back to 1724) sticking out from a sea of hard lava rock. More than 200 people, taking refuge in the church, were buried alive in it. The site is now a national park.

The Mayon Volcano is a popular trekking site. The intrepid go for an entire climb, top to bottom, which takes a couple of days. The less energetic can drive 48 km to the **Mayon Vista Lodge** at 770 metres, a 10-room hotel run by the Philippine Tourism Atuhority. The drive takes about one and a half hours from Legazpi City.

Chocolate Hills

In the **Central Visayas** is **Bohol Island**, know a primarily for its mysterious **Chocolate Hills**. Tagbilaran is the main city and its Baclayon Church, dating from 1595, is one of the most venerable in the country. The city has a selection of nice beaches and a few beach resorts. It is the site of the blood pact between Legazpi and a native chieftain, Datu Sikatuna. But the main interest of the island centres on the Chocolate Hills, so-called because they are brown in summer, though they could just as easily have been called "green hills" for their colour during other times of the year!

There are literally hundreds of the perfectly cone-shaped mounds, the largest rising to about 300 metres. For those visitors with time — they are only 55 km northeast of **Tagbilaran**, near the town of **Carmen** — there is the **Chocolate Hills Resort** atop one of the highest hills. The view is marvellous and you can sit and meditate on how these bizarre mounds came to be.

Palawan

The most south eastern fringe of the Philippine archipelago is the **Palawan Island** group. Though originally spotted by Magellan's historian, Pigafetta, in the 16th century, the islands remained firmly in the possession of the Sultans of Jolo and Borneo until the 19th century. The Chinese traders of old knew the islands and the name is supposedly derived from *Pa Lao Yu* ("Land of Beautiful Safe Harbour").

In spite of comprising a quarter of the entire Philippine islands and being only an hour away from Manila on a PAL jet, the islands were long ignored until the advent of "black gold" strikes of 1976. After oil was discovered, Palawan became the centre for exploration which at one time was supplying 17 percent of the country's needs.

With the discovery of the "Tabon skull" (circa 22,000 BC), the islands also became known as the "Cradle of Philippines Civilisation." Two-thirds of the 29 Tabon caves, located 34 metres up on the western face of **Lipuon Point**, have been excavated.

One of the rarest sites is **St. Paul' Subterrranean National Park**, a 3,901 hectare area with limestone and marble cliffs, the "St Paul's" refers to cathedral-like underground caverns through which an underground river flows for about five kilometres, eventually emptying into the South China Sea. Only small *bancas* can negotiate the mouth of the cave and the lighting in the pitch black cavern is by kerosene or carbide lamps.

Mysterious mounds dot the island of Bohol, where these "chocolate hills" (so-named because they turn brown in the heat of summer) are the main tourist attraction.

Travellers Tips

Transport

All lines of transportation to any section of the country emanate from the country's hub, Manila. Most visitors fly because it is quicker and Philippine Airlines, the country's domestic (as well as international) carrier blankets the country with its air routes. For those with more time, it is possible to take a train, a freighter, a cruiseliner, a bus or even a car, or any combination and see the country.

Buses: From the various private terminals around the city, buses head out to just about every corner of Luzon. All of the main tourist centres — Baguio and the North, the coastal area of La Union and points north, the resorts of Paganjan and Batangas, are all accessible by bus.

Trains: There are only two railway lines out of Manila. One runs from Manila to San Fernando in La Union province, the beautiful coastal area north of Manila, from where you can continue north by road or head up into the mountains to Baguio or Banaue. There are four trains a day for the six-hour journey with air-conditioned (₱65), tourist (₱45) and economy (₱40) classes. The other route runs south to Legazpi City from where you can enjoy the beauty of the Mayon Volcano and the Bicol area. There are three trains a day leaving for the 14-hour journey to Camalig, from where you take a short bus ride to Legazpi City. The most comfortable is the air-conditioned "Mayon Express" which leaves every night at 7pm, arriving at 9:10 the next morning. ₱85 plus ₱60 for sleepers. On the other trains, tourist class is ₱75 and economy ₱50. All trains leave from Manila's Tutuban railroad station in Binondo.

Cruiseliners. The **Dona Monserrat** is the only cruiseliner regularly operating in the archipelago. Bookings and schedules through any travel agent.

Freighters. There are two centres for inter-island shipping, Manila and Cebu. There are regular runs each week and it is quite possible to plan a scheduled itinerary. Most of the Manila daily papers carry the shipping schedules but the Manila *Bulletin* probably has the best and easiest to read. Bookings can be done by phone directly or through travel agents.

Student discounts: They are available on all forms of bus, plane and shipping transportation but identification is necessary. Check with the **Youth & Travel Association of the Philippines** (YSTAPHIL), 2456 Tave Ave., Malate. Tel: 59-9821. The organisation issues discount cards and has other tour and travel discounts.

Major Airlines

Air France
Manila Hilton, U.N. Avenue, Metro Manila.
Tel: 599241

Air Niugini
Philippine Village Hotel, Pasay City, Metro Manila.
Tel: 807131/804738

British Airways
Ermita Centre Bldg., 1350 Roxas Blvd., Metro Manila.
Tel: 507611

Cathay Pacific Airways
Ermita Centre Bldg., Roxas Blvd., Metro Manila.
Tel: 507611

China Airlines
Hotel Filipinas Annex, Roxas Blvd., Metro Manila.
Tel: 590086

Japan Airlines
Bayview Plaza Hotel, Roxas Blvd., Metro Manila.
Tel: 505611/505610

KLM Royal Dutch Airlines
Philamlife Bldg., U.N. Avenue, Metro Manila.
Tel: 582061

Korean Airlines
Bayview Plaza Hotel, Roxas Blvd., Metro Manila.
Tel: 504365

Malaysian Airlines System
Manila Hilton, U.N. Avenue, Metro Manila.
Tel: 586893/586909

Pakistan International Airlines
Suite 809, L&S Bldg., 1515 Roxas Blvd., Metro Manila.
Tel: 500091

Pan American Airways
Delgado Bldg., Bonifacio Drive, Port Area, Metro Manila.
Tel: 492161/471981

Philippine Airlines
Vernida Bldg., Legazpi St., Legazpi Village, Metro Manila.
Tel: 81061
1515 Roxas Blvd,. Metro Minila.
Tel: 584705

Qantas Airways
1148 Roxas Blvd., Metro Manila.
Tel: 599081

Sabena
Manila Hilton, U.N. Avenue, Metro Manila.
Tel: 508636

Scandinavian Airline System
Domestic Insurance Bldg,. Bonifacio Drive, Port Area, Metro Manila.
Tel: 483516

Singapore Airlines
Magsaysay Bldg., 250 T.M. Kalaw, Ermita, Metro Manila.
Tel: 506606

Swissair
Silahis International Hotel Bldg., 1990 Roxas Blvd., Metro Manila.
Tel: 507641

Thai Airways International
Domestic Insurance Bldg., Bonifacio

Drive, Port Area, Metro Manila.
Tel: 484014

Air India.
Manila Hilton, U.N. Avenue, Metro
Manila.
Tel: 508757

Alitalia
1022 Roxas Blvd., Metro Manila.
Tel: 582091

American Airlines
Manila Hilton, U.N. Avenue, Metro
Manila.
Tel: 500413

Canadian Pacific Airlines
Pacific Bank Bldg., Ayala Avenue,
Makati, Metro Manila.
Tel: 898531

Lufthansa
J.P. Laurel Memorial Foundation Bldg.,
Pedro Gil Cor. Roxas Blvd., Ermita,
Metro Manila
Tel: 599251

*Out in the provinces, you can still see
horse-drawn calesas such as this one.*

Major Embassies

Australia
3rd Floor Chinabank Bank Bldg, Paseo de Roxas Makati, Metro Manila.
Tel: 874961

Austria
SGV Building Ayala Avenue Makati, Metro Manila.
Tel: 893011

Belgium
6th floor, Don Sacinto Bldg, de la Rosa cor. Salcedo Sts., Legaspi Village, Makati, Metro Manila.
Tel: 876571-74

Canada
4th Flr PAL Bldg Ayala Avenue Makati, Metro Manila.
Tel: 876536; 877846

China, People's Republic of
4896 Pasay Road, Dasmariñas Village, Makati, Metro Manila.
Tel: 853148/867715

Denmark
10th flr, Citibank Center, 8741 Paseo de Noxas, Makati, Metro Manila.
Tel: 856756/857196

Finland
1386 Palm Ave., Dasmariñas Village, Makati, Metro Manila.
Tel: 898934/895924

France
2nd Flr Filipinas Life Bldg 6786, Ayala Avenue Makati Metro Manila.
Tel: 876561-63

Germany
Citibank Center Bldg Paseo de Roxas, Makati Metro Manila.
Tel: 864900; 864906; 864909

Greece
Antonino Bldg T M Kalaw St, Metro Manila.
Tel: 580911; 583355

India
7th Floor, Casmer Bldg, Salcedo St., Legaspi Village, Makati, Metro Manila.
Tel: 872445/873339

Ireland
1195 Maria Orosa St. Ermita, Metro Manila.
Tel: 500505; 502712

Israel
Metrobank Bldg 6813 Ayala Ave Makati, Metro Manila.
Tel: 885329

Italy
Zeta Building 1191 Salcedo St. Legaspi Village Makati Metro Manila.
Tel: 887843; 887137

Japan
375 Buendia Aue. Ext., Makati Metro Manila.
Tel: 891836-39

Malaysia
2nd flr., D.K.A. Bldg., Gallardo cor Jordesillas Sts., Salcedo Village, Makati, Metro Manila.
Tel: 874576-78

Mexico
814 Pasay Road San Lorenzo Village, Makati Metro Manila.
Tel: 857263; 857323

Netherlands
6th Flr Metrobank Bldg Ayala Avenue, Makati Metro Manila.
Tel: 887768; 851516; 887753

Norway
Suite 603, Erechem Bldg. Salcedo cor. Hernera Sts., Legaspi Village, Makati, Metro Manila.
Tel: 881111

Pakistan
CMI Bldg Ayala Avenue Makati, Metro Manila.
Tel: 882776; 882772; 885854

Portugal
814 Pasay Road Makati Metro Manila.
Tel: 873939

Soviet Union
1245 Acacia Rd., Dasmariñas Village, Makati, Metro Manila.
Tel: 859690/859645

A statue of the Filipino warrior Lapu-lapu in Mactan Island near Cebu City. This local hero was the first Filipino to take up arms against Magellan.

Singapore
ODC International Plaza, 219 Salcedo St
Legaspi Village Makati, Metro Manila.
Tel: 894596; 851865

Spain
2515 L Guinto St Metro Manila.
Tel: 582885; 596676-79

Sweden
8th Floor Citibank Center, 8741 Paseo
de Roxas Makati Metro Manila.
Tel: 882510; 885122

Switzerland
140 Amorsolo St Makati Metro Manila.
Tel: 865591-92

Thailand
603 Oledan Building, 131 Ayala Avenue
Makati Metro Manila.
Tel: 876491; 876496

United Kingdom
Electra House, 115-117 Esteban St.,
Legaspi Village, Makati, Metro Manila
Tel: 891051

United States of America
Roxas Blvd Metro Manila.
Tel: 598011

Documents

Passport
It is necessary to have a valid passport
before entering The Philippines. Special
entry permits obtainable from the
Philippine Consulate are required for
holders of official Hongkong and Taipei
identity cards.

Visa
Visitors, except those from countries with
which The Philippines has no diplomatic
relations, stateless persons and nationals
from restricted countries, may enter the
country without visas and may stay for
21 up to 54 days provided they hold an
onward or return ticket. 21 days is
normal. To extend one's stay a visitor
may apply with the Commission on
Immigration and Department for a visa,
valid for 59 days but extendable for
varying periods up to a total of one year.
Visas issued before arrival are valid for
59 days.

Note: Tourists arriving at the Manila
International Airport should ask the
Immigration Officer on duty for a
"Tourist Visitor Transient" Pass, which
is supposed to be given to every tourist at
immigration but rarely is. This slip which
has your name on it, usually ensures a
speedy passage through customs.

Health Regulations

Valid international stamp for cholera,
only if passing through an infected area,
and smallpox, only if reinstated by the
World Health Organisation.

Currency

There is no limit on foreign currency

being imported into The Philippines. However, foreign currency to be taken out must not exceed the amount brought in. There is now a currency declaration regarding Philippine pesos, tourists and non-residents may bring into or out of the Philippines ₱500.

The Philippine Peso (100 centavos) is the official monetary unit. Coins are in one, five, ten, twenty five, fifty centavo and one peso denominations. Five peso coins are also available.
Bills are in two, five, ten, twenty, fifty and hundred peso denominations.

Rate of exchange fluctuates from ₱7.30 to ₱7.50 per us$1.

Other currencies convertible to the

Philippine peso are: Canadian Dollars, Italian Lire, Dutch Guilders, Australian Dollars, British Pounds, West German Marks, Swiss Francs, Japanese Yen, Austrian Schillings, French Francs, Hongkong Dollars and Singapore Dollars.

Travelers cheques may be cashed in all commercial banks in The Philippines. They are also acceptable in most hotels, restaurants and shops.

Aside from banks and hotels, foreign currency may also be converted at money exchanges, tourist shops and some restaurants.

*A great place for people-watching —
Luneta Park on a Sunday afternoon.*

Conversion Rates (1981)

US Dollar	₱ 7.95
Australian Dollar	9.14
Canadian Dollar	9.54
Deutchmark	3.35
French Franc	1.40
Italian Lira	0.0076
Japanese Yen	0.0356
Netherlands Guilder	3.018
Pounds Sterling	15.88
Swiss Franc	3.89
Hongkong Dollar	1.44
Singapore Dollar	3.73

Visitors are advised to exchange their foreign currencies into Philippine pesos only with outlets authorized by the Central Bank of the Philippines. Authorized exchange counters can be found in banks, hotels, travel agencies, restaurants, savings and loan associations and tourists shops. **Always demand a Central Bank receipt which you will be needing when shopping at Duty-Free Shops.**

Credit Cards

Cards widely honoured are American Express, Bank Americard, Carte Blanche, Diners Club, Eurocard, and Master Charge. Hotels belonging to international chains have their own house cards.

Electricity

In Manila the power supply is 220 volts A.C., 60 cycles. Most hotels would also have 110 volt capability. There are frequent "brown-outs" in Manila.

Filipino Medicine

Faith healers: Though officially condemned by the Philippines Medical Association and similarly vilified abroad, faith healers exist throughout the country and are doing very well, thank you. There are even packaged "faith healing tours." Through spiritual concentration, faith healers are said to be able to "extract"

the "trouble" or "pain" or "problem" without ever cutting the body open. "Blood" also appears from these non-wounds. Proceed at your own risk.

Telephones

Local calls are 40 centavos (40¢) but you may have a problem finding enough 10¢ pieces. Public phones are red. Rather than give change, most people just let you use their phones. Most hotels charge their guests for local phone calls and have pay phones in the lobby. Most international calls can usually be made very quickly from Manila, but are much slower in the provinces. Long distance domestic calls, from Manila or from the provinces, may take some time, depending on where you are. Patience is needed with telephone calls in Manila, especially to the Makati business area, as exchanges become overloaded and the engaged signal sounds after the first few numbers. New exchanges are being put in and the system is improving from the days when it was very overloaded.

Business Hours

Government and private offices maintain regular working hours from 8:00am to 5:00pm. Some offices, however, open at 9:00am and close at 6:00pm.

Stock Exchanges

Three exchanges operate in the Philippine stock market: The Manila, Makati and Metropolitan stock exchanges. Trading hours are from 9:30am to 1:30pm, Monday to Friday.

Etiquette & Customs

Shaking hands is the customary form of greeting for both men and women in The Philippines. An expression of respect among Filipinos is to take the right hand of an elder and touch it to the forehead. Visitors are not expected to do this. A form of address not unusual amongst

Filipinos is to call a person by his or her profession, for instance a lawyer might be addressed as Attorney, even in social circumstances. Engineers, architects, etc. are addressed by their profession in conversation and in writing. Government officials are also addressed by their titles such as Assemblyman, Minister, Director, etc.

Tipping

Tipping is an accepted practice with 10 percent being standard. However, many establishments have adopted a 10 percent service charge, so, whatever is left behind on the plate is extra. Additional tipping is optional. Tipping taxi drivers is also optional.

Major Hotels in Manila

Century Park Sheraton
Vito Cruz cor M Adriatico, Malate, Metro Manila.
Tel: 506-041

Holiday Inn
1700 Roxas Blvd, Pasay City.
Tel: 597-961

Hyatt Regency Manila
2702 Roxas Blvd, Metro Manila.
Tel: 802-611

Manila Garden Hotel
Makati, Metro Manila.
Tel: 857-911

Manila Hilton
United Nations Avenue, Ermita, Metro Manila.
Tel: 573-711

Manila Hotel
Rizal Park, Metro Manila.
Tel: 470-011

Manila Intercontinental
Makati Commercial Centre, Metro Manila.
Tel: 894-011

Manila Mandarin
cor Makati Ave & Paseo de Roxas, Metro Manila.
Tel: 85-78-11

Manila Peninsula
cor Makati & Ayala Ave, Metro Manila.
Tel: 85-77-11

Philippine Plaza
Cultural Centre Complex, Roxas Blvd, Metro Manila.
Tel: 59-37-11

Silahis International
1990 Roxas Blvd, Metro Manila.
Tel: 57-38-11

El Grande/Tropical Palace
Phase IV BF Homes, Paranaque Rizal.
Tel: 827-10-11

Mirador
1000 San Marcelino, Ermita, Metro Manila.
Tel: 57-49-11

One of Manila's many international-standard hotels, the Silahis International

Index